Sunshine in Mourning

A look back on the first year without you.

Harley Firth

For Kristi,

You were

my

everything.

Love,

H

Sunshine in Mourning

There was a light breeze in the air on June 10th. It carried with it the familiar scents and sounds of summer: fresh cut grass, sunscreen, and the familiar song of water, flowing over the rocks of the waterfall in our little piece of paradise. On what would have otherwise been an oppressively hot day, the breeze was welcomingly cool. It made its rounds through haphazard knots of people scattered around the yard: Aunts and Uncles, sisters and brothers. Even friends, coworkers, neighbors, and acquaintances; all were family, today.

My Aunt and Uncle sat in the shade of the house while speaking with our neighbors, Jim and John, "the two J's" as I sometimes jokingly referred to them. A group of business colleagues chatted with my sister-in-law and nieces, one studying for her upcoming CPA, and the other pursuing a doctorate in physical therapy. Friends from our old neighborhood gathered around the firepit, sharing stories of times that now seem so long ago. On any other day, in any other setting, perhaps, such an eclectic gathering would be truly peculiar to behold; today, however, it made an odd kind of sense.

That's just who Kristi was.

I found myself looking around, stunned, as I came to a realization: I didn't know her as well as I thought I had. I didn't know my quiet, unassuming, bashful, even introverted wife was a giant among her friends. I didn't know just how many people loved her like I did. I didn't know, until now, that you don't need to raise your voice to be heard; you can do it by simply being there, just as Kristi was.

Over and over, as I greeted people and eavesdropped on conversations— unable to bring myself to join, just yet—and uncomfortably moved from person to person, thanking them for being present, there was one common theme: Kristi was the kind of person who simply made others feel comfortable, important, special. I thought of her smile: the kind of smile that could bring up the temperature in an otherwise cold or dreary room. It was that smile, that warmth, which had gathered so many people here today.

At that moment, I felt that my heart, while broken, was full. Full of love, and, yes, full of sadness. But also, full of appreciation and, in some strange way, a feeling I hadn't expected to feel again: joy.

I'm not a "believer," and you would be hard pressed to get me to step foot into a church unless they were offering free food and drinks; but I do believe that everyone carries an energy, and that energy does not disappear when we die. Kristi's energy was with us that day, and she continues to be with us every day in the little things that surround us. It is in the birds she loved to watch. In my dogs, Sally and Jake. In the air we breathe, and in what makes other people good. My wife had an energy that I will never, ever be able to replicate, and will never be able to forget. Her ability to keep me calm, to keep my tempest from raging, as it so often did, was there that day. I don't know how to thank her for that, but I'm sure she knows how grateful I am.

I realized, that day, that this is not where her story ends. My wife's impact on the world, and on myself, was far greater than I had ever imagined, and would continue long past her death. Today, we were not here to mourn her death.

We were here to celebrate her life.

"People are like stained-glass windows. They sparkle and shine when the sun is out, but when the darkness

sets in, their true beauty is revealed only if there is a light from within." -Kubler-Ross

---

I've never really accepted loss until now. I've never owned it until now. It has never ached in my bones until now. And yet, it has become a consuming fire within me that needs to be respected, appreciated, and most of all, honored. Loss is not something to take lightly; it is something that must be allowed full access to your mind, body, and spirit. The results are terrifying. I have cried rivers. I have been wracked with sorrow. I have laughed at memories. I have been sullen and removed. I have drunk heavily, eaten poorly, and allowed anger to distract me because that was the only emotion available. I have lost, and now I am trying to be found.

It's been over 365 days since Kristi died, and in that time, I have memorialized her, idolized her, given her back to the world, written countless words and lines about her, and tried my best to forge a path forward, a path that gets me to the place where I belong. It isn't about her anymore; now it's about me, and all the things she taught me, all the things she gave me, and how I decide to use them.

It's hard to explain what happens to someone's brain during the grieving process. It's almost as if you turn into a different person that continues to morph, change, step forward, fall back, and eventually grow as the months pass. At first, I was the doer, getting all of the things that needed to be taken care of - done properly. After that, sadness and desperation set in, at which point it was time for me to take off on my journey. I began to see that there were these glimmers of light at the end of the tunnel, despite not knowing how long the tunnel was.

Let me tell you now, the tunnel is long. It is winding. It is filled with intersections, and the range of emotions and feelings towards people in my life (and hers) has varied immensely from day-to-day and week-to-week. I don't believe I've learned to love any better, but at this point I certainly have learned how to turn from anger and simply walk away. I have been cursed at and scorned by the very same people who praised me for everything I did during Kristi's illness, and the days and weeks leading up to her death. I have been called names that don't bear repeating, and have even been accused of being selfish, when all I have ever been is generous.

But this story is not about them. This story is the story of my wife, and how losing her has become a quest for me to find little pieces of her in everything I do. My goal in writing is not to pour my heart out to the world for sympathy or for pity. My goal here is to have a discussion. To start a dialogue about my grieving process, and all of its intricacies, so others can see that grieving is not meant to be a purely sorrowful event in our lives, but that it is a pathway from loss to happiness. That grieving can be a cathartic and amazing process if we allow ourselves to be immersed in it, and that the pathway is different for everyone. That there truly is sunshine in mourning.

I do not believe grief needs to be permanent; rather, I believe that we can use loss to define a better future, that the person we have lost wants a bright future for us, and that getting stuck in one stage of grief or another is simply the universe's way of giving us the time needed to absorb and understand some part of our loss before we can move on. I'm not going to pretend to know how many stages of grief there really are or aren't, but I do know this:

I've fallen so many times I don't know how I keep getting up, but I also smile, I laugh, and I stare at her picture—not painfully, wondering what could have been, but remembering what was. I believe this keeps me whole, and I also believe each of these stumbles has incredible value. In falling, I get to feel what it's like to have lost, what it's like to acknowledge that loss, and then when the tears have dried, I must climb back up to my feet. In the end, the climb is what's important - because without it there won't be a future.

So, if you've fallen...sit there for a minute, gather your senses, and hold onto that space until you're comfortable letting go. Then, lift yourself up, dry your cheeks, and keep moving forward into the day, because that's where your future lies.

"Grief can destroy you --or focus you. You can decide a relationship was all for nothing if it had to end in death, and you alone. OR you can realize that every moment of it had more meaning than you dared to recognize at the time, so much meaning it scared you, so you just lived, just took for granted the love and laughter of each day, and didn't allow yourself to consider the sacredness of it. — Dean Koontz, Odd Hours.

The Terror of Diagnosis

December 28, 2012 was a typical day in Illinois. Cold, but not too much so, and not enough snow on the ground to really call it winter. Kristi had received a call from her breast doctor the day before saying that they needed to do a chest and abdomen CT. Her annual breast MRI had "picked something up," and they wanted to look at it more closely.

She was nervous, but not overly. She had had a complete hysterectomy 13 months prior, to ensure her risk of breast and ovarian cancer were greatly reduced. Kristi, like her mother and Aunt, had the BRCA1 gene mutation, which significantly increased her risk of breast and ovarian cancer, and was very proactive in making sure her chances of getting cancer were reduced. The hysterectomy was the first step in what we assumed would be a long lifetime of monitoring and caution.

We arrived at the doctor's office late in the afternoon. It was dark as we walked across the parking lot to the building and made our way upstairs. It seems surreal now, but I recall Christmas decorations in the lobby, waiting to be taken down until after the new year, as if to extend that warmth and cheer as long as possible in a place so frequently barren of it.

The office was empty but for the receptionist at the front desk. It was, after all, the Friday before New Year's Eve. We could tell something was wrong by the way we were asked to take a seat immediately in one of the smaller meeting rooms. This wasn't going to be a quick CT follow up. The room was quiet, the bland office furniture careful not to give away any of it secrets. How many times had it heard the dreaded words, "You've got cancer"?

After a few short moments, we both became nervous. Kristi is not one to hide her emotions, and I could see her fear in the stiffness of her shoulders, the crease in her brows. I knew she was afraid of being diagnosed with breast cancer. Her mother had been diagnosed twice, and as a result had been fighting one form of cancer or another for what seemed like years. But, what about the hysterectomy? Wasn't that supposed to minimize the chances for breast cancer in a BRCA1 patient? Little did we know, it wasn't breast cancer at all.

Dr. Lee appeared shortly thereafter. Despite trying to remain professional, she entered slowly, closed the door carefully, with the look of someone carrying a tremendous weight. She and Kristi had known each other for years, and as with everyone, she adored my wife.

She walked across the room, held Kristi's hand, and told her what was going on inside of her. The CT scan had revealed multiple tumors in her uterine cavity, and a host of smaller tumors ravaging their way through her abdomen all the way to her diaphragm. This was not breast cancer at all; it was ovarian, or peritoneal cancer, and it was very aggressive.

The shock of hearing the words "you've got cancer" spoken to your wife is nothing short of debilitating. You don't simply hear them as much as you receive them, as you would a physical blow. My mind reeled from the sudden knowledge, my stomach twisted in an effort to avoid vomiting. My heart and lungs felt squeezed tight, as if some giant from mythical tales had settled on top of my chest. I do not know if I have ever felt so helpless.

After recovering from the shock and wiping away the tears, we were given the name of a gynecologic oncologist and told to reach out to her the following week. It was late on Friday December 28th; a holiday weekend, with New Year's Eve on the following Monday.

I cannot describe the collective panic between Kristi and I at that moment. The drive home was filled with questions, tears, and a horrible sense of dread. There is no terror quite as real as being diagnosed with a cancer you don't understand how you contracted, and don't know how to fight. No frustration so intense as helplessly watching your wife beg for her life to a God you don't believe in. Still, I am amazed at how well Kristi managed, given everything she knew, everything she had experienced with breast and ovarian cancer. Her Aunt lost her life to ovarian cancer some 30 years prior, and memories of her Aunt's suffering must have danced in Kristi's head like out of control marionettes hell-bent on taking her own.

After a tear-soaked weekend filled with phone calls, internet searches, moments of panic, and hours of simply holding onto one another, help came in the name of Dr. Barbara Buttin: a tiny, soft-spoken Gynecologic Oncologist we met with that first week in January. She explained the situation, and recommended surgery and chemotherapy as the first course of action. We immediately scheduled Kristi's surgery, and she was quickly put at ease. As we talked about the future on the way home from that appointment, I could see hope in her eyes once again. It wasn't so much the fact that we now had someone in our corner, but that she believed in that person. Kristi's relationship with Dr. Buttin became a source of comfort for her over the course of her treatments and beyond. For that, I can never thank her enough.

Kristi's procedure, called a "debulking surgery," lasted more than seven hours. I am not sure what I was expecting, but seven hours seemed like an awfully long time, even for such an intense procedure. The hours stretched on for days, it seemed, and I found myself making small talk with three of Kristi's friends who were there with me, thumbing through my phone to find some source of distraction on the internet, messaging friends and family with updates, and at times, staring at the surgical board for no reason at all. A part of me knew the surgery would be a success, but as calm as I may have seemed, the fear of failure hovered like a banshee around my shoulders, whispering all the dreaded "what-ifs."

Finally, the exhausted surgeons returned, and after Kristi and I reunited, Dr. Buttin and Dr. Shoup, the head of the Surgical Oncology Team, came to explain the results. We discovered there were two large tumors in her uterine cavity that needed to be removed. There were also tumors surrounding a portion of her colon, a portion of her gallbladder, a portion of her liver, and along her diaphragm. All of these tumors, including portions of each organ needed to be carefully removed. Carcinomatosis, small tumors shaped like grains of rice, had spread throughout her entire abdomen, and Dr. Buttin and Dr. Shoup had spent hours hunting them down and removing them one by one.

This was the first battle of a long War.

After the surgery Dr. Buttin admitted Kristi to the ICU, where she began her recovery. Her body had been beaten and bruised, she was groggy and confused, but just the sight of her lifted my spirits. She was alive. There were some initial complications after the surgery, but the team in the ICU were incredibly responsive and amazing at their jobs, and in a few days, Kristi was ready to be released and begin the next step: eradicating any remaining cancer cells the surgeons were unable to find and remove.

During her stay in the ICU, friends and family visited, and her optimism through it all helped lift me up and give me hope. We just knew that if we did it together we could win. Yes, we looked at the statistics – you can't avoid them. We knew the odds were daunting, to say the least. But we also knew that if we didn't keep our spirits up, the war was already lost. Many nights we were wracked with tears. There were days when her fatigue was so great I often wondered if she was going to make it. There were setbacks, but even through the worst of them we always attempted to look at things in a positive fashion.

After three weeks of recovery at home, Kristi began treatment with chemotherapy. Unlike normal chemotherapy, which is traditionally injected into your arm, or a port in your chest, Kristi's chemotherapy was intraperitoneal. In layman's terms, the cancer-fighting infusion was to be injected directly into her abdomen. The success rates for this type of treatment are higher, as it attacks the cancer cells that remain after surgery in a much more direct fashion, and very often patients go a longer period of time before the cancer returns.

We were unbelievably hopeful this treatment would work. We knew that it could knock the cancer back for months, and maybe even years. We began to hope again, and even, tentatively, to plan for the future.

Unfortunately, life did not conform to those hopes.

The aggressive treatment caused other complications, and the formation of a fistula in Kristi's lower intestine, which in turn forced her to stop this type of infusion. It also forced the doctors to temporarily reroute Kristi's colon, and she underwent treatment to be given a colostomy bag. This was a nightmare come to life for my wife. For four to five weeks we struggled trying to get the proper fit, trying to keep it hidden, making sure it did not leak or give off any odor, and always trying to maintain her dignity. Throughout all this she continued with standard chemotherapy infusions, and much to everyone's amazement, her life. I became the only person she would trust to help her with her colostomy, and slowly, over time, we developed a pattern that worked. We even laughed at a few of the mishaps that invariably happen when dealing with a device poorly designed for its intended role.

None of this was easy, but these are the things you do to give your wife the sense of self and dignity she needs to go on with each day. It was simply inconceivable that I would watch her struggle with something like this and not do everything I could to help. At every opportunity I assured her that living with a colostomy was significantly better than not living at all. This was not the kind of role I ever expected to play, but one that I would gladly do over again. The ability to provide this kind of comfort to the person your life revolves around is an absolute must for male caregivers. Yes, we can be strong. Yes, we can be masculine. But in the end, we are nothing more than husbands, sons, fathers, friends, and brothers, would-be heroes in the face of a monster we cannot fight, if we don't adapt.

As a husband, there is sense of helplessness that comes with a cancer diagnosis in the person you love, the person whose life and love you revolve around as constant and steady as the moon. You cannot change the course of history. You have no control over the disease, and in many ways, there is very little you can do about the emotional reactions and anxiety your spouse will have throughout the course of treatment and recovery. Some days are simply there to get through, while others will test your ability to understand, your desire to fix things, and in the quiet of the night after everyone has gone to sleep, you will invariably throw your hands in the air as if to say, "Okay, you win." Then you will wake up in the morning as if nothing has happened and care for your wife.

Cancer is terrifying. An invisible enemy, infiltrating your home, your life, mindless and bent on the destruction of all that you hold dear, things you thought infallible, things you took for granted. It is relentless. I soon discovered that my role, my purpose, was to minimize Kristi's stress, reduce her anxiety, provide some level of home nursing, and to be her biggest fan, cheerleader, and day to day caregiver. How do you do this? What things need to change? How do you respond to different situations? I had to learn all of this first hand. I know I made many mistakes, but like a soldier who has been given a field promotion, you learn as you go. There is no turning back.

And the learning is hard. The technical things came easy, but the emotional, and even spiritual elements were more difficult. How do you stay positive? How do you suppress your intense frustration at people who are praying to God for your wife to get better, when by all logic it was that very same God who allowed her to get sick in the first place? How do you comfort someone when you are as scared as they are? How do you watch someone who is fighting for their life break down in tears because they are furious and terrified of the roll of the dice life has given them? None of it is simple, but when you love someone like I loved Kristi, you find a way to do what needs to be done.

My other job during all of this was to be unerringly aware of what was going on with my wife's health, with her treatment, with the house, and with her life. How was she feeling? Was she eating enough? How was her emotional state? Was she getting enough rest? These, and so many other questions needed to be asked on a daily, weekly, and monthly basis. My life had always been centered around doing things for people. I'm not a natural nurturer; I'm a problem solver, a person who Gets Things Done. Changing the way I thought about and approached life was a huge challenge for me. Thankfully, my love for Kristi was so much deeper than the emotional and psychological battle I was waging, that at no point did I ever even consider doing things differently. It was all I could do, so I did it with everything I had.

"It's only when we truly know and understand that we have a limited time on earth - and that we have no way of knowing when our time is up, we will then begin to live each day to the fullest, as if it was the only one we had." -Kubler-Ross

---

Kristi made it through the first round of chemotherapy, and over time, she and I mastered the colostomy. And after several months she was approved for surgery to reverse the bypass of her colon. Like any surgery, we entered this one with some trepidation, as we were concerned about the possible formation of a hernia, which was common, after the surgery was complete. This was a risk she was willing to take, but, as luck would have it, our fears were justified. After several months a hernia did appear. At first, this wasn't such a big deal, although it did cause some issues for Kristi in terms of the appearance of her stomach; but we would joke that her stomach was already scarred enough that this didn't really matter. For the most part she managed, altered her wardrobe slightly, and those who didn't know her had no idea it even existed because it wasn't even noticeable through her clothes. Unfortunately, that little hernia would come back to haunt us a few years later.

Over the course of the next three years Kristi would transition several times between various chemotherapy treatments, surgeries, remission, and the inevitable planning to be in treatment again when test results indicated its return like an unwelcome guest at a party. This is what ovarian cancer does; just when you think you've got an edge, and you're doing okay, it comes back. You can never rest. You can never let down your guard. You are always on alert, always wondering when it's going to return, and where. For many women it isn't a case of "if," it truly is a case of "when." And for most women, the "when" is far too soon, and with devastating effect.

The moments of stress were many, and dealing with those was no easy task. The day before her CA-125 exam, a blood test particularly effective in predicting the presence of tumors in patients with a high risk of ovarian cancer, was a particularly stressful time for Kristi. This marker was an indicator of whether cancer was present or not, and any number above 35 wasn't good. The higher the number, the more cancer was likely present. The sheer terror of having the test done was enough to make her break down and cry at times. Adding onto this the regularly-scheduled CT scans, breast MRI's, and mammograms was almost too much to bear, because every test brings with it the fear of being diagnosed with a recurrence. In truth, despite her outward smile and beauty, she lived in a state of fear the entirety of the time she was in treatment.

As I look back, I honestly don't know how she did it. Every day she got out of bed, showered, put on makeup, did her hair and did her absolute best to look like someone who wasn't in a life and death battle with cancer. And she fooled the world. Even during those weeks and months when she had no hair, she always looked her best. Even though it may have taken more than half of the energy she had just to get up, she never let the cancer take away her beauty or her grace. It may have taken away her strength, her ability to live quietly, almost invisibly, but it never took who she was. I look back on those days now in awe of how she maintained a smile. Of how she worried more about her sons than herself. How she tried to be not only the best mother, but the best wife, friend, daughter, and sister anyone could ever ask for. Kristi was the kind of person others wish they could be.

I don't know what I did right or wrong during this time. But I was there for my wife. I cried with her, and I held her hand. I told her I loved her every single day. I cared for her when she needed help, and even when she didn't. We did all the things she needed to do to feel alive and in doing them I was alive. We travelled to see family, vacationed as often as possible, enjoyed time with friends, and attended as many of her sons' college sporting and life events as possible. We lived life for her, and if there was ever anything she wanted to do, I did my best to make it possible. I will never know if it was enough, but I am hopeful it was.

Some of this wasn't easy; in fact, some of it was unbelievably painful. But we attempted to pretend like the hourglass hadn't tipped over as often as humanly possible. It was, perhaps, one of the gifts I was able to give her, without even intending to. I let her believe—or, maybe I let us both believe—that she would live forever.

"Mourning is the process of moving from fantasy to acceptance. You may always miss your loved one, but you can also relearn to enjoy life in the present." - Jonathan Grayson

---

In December of 2016 Kristi was in treatment for her fourth recurrence. There was a small tumor contained inside a hernia sac in her abdomen, and it needed to be eradicated. That same hernia Kristi was worried about in 2013 had become a problem again three years later. Available treatment options were becoming more and more limited, and she was enrolled in a clinical trial with a standard chemotherapy regimen. The initial results of the chemotherapy looked positive and the tumor began to shrink, but after a few months and a 40% reduction in the tumor's size, the results bottomed out, and her CA-125 began to soar. The chemotherapy had become ineffective, and we once again had to sit down with Dr. Buttin and her team to look at new options.

She was given the opportunity to take a new drug recently approved by the FDA, called a PARP inhibitor. This drug is designed to inhibit a protein that BRCA1 cancers need in order to grow. The drug, Lynparza, was so effective in trials that we assumed we would see a 18 to 20-month extension of Kristi's life, with the hope that immunotherapy and other new advanced treatments would be ready down the road at the next, almost inevitable recurrence. I had been watching the news and reading reports on Lynparza for years. It was described as a major advance in the treatment of ovarian cancer, so our belief that this would help rid her of any cancer was justified; or, so we thought.

To everyone's amazement, the Lynparza had absolutely no effect. After 6 weeks of ineffectual treatment, Kristi's cancer was now growing, and the tumor in the hernia sac needed to be slowed down. She was offered the opportunity to enter into a trial at Northwestern Hospital in Chicago, but the washout time to rid her body of the Lynparza was three weeks, meaning she would not be under any treatment, and would have unabated cancer growth during this time. Although we knew her cancer was growing and definitely spreading, we had no other choice but to agree to the washout. We were nervous, but she was being treated by the best doctors in Chicago; we didn't think three weeks would hurt her chances of survival.

Kristi and I consulted with a new team of Oncologists at Northwestern in Chicago and she began the immunotherapy treatment in early April of 2017. We were nervous, but optimistic. Would the treatment work?

Would the tumors shrink? How much time did she have left? A year, six months? We knew we were now counting time, but we didn't know the unit of measure. It was Easter weekend, and there was nothing to celebrate. Her sister came to visit for a few days. We discussed how much time we thought we had left with her and agreed that however much time it was, we were going to make the best of it. We were going to plan trips, create a sort of bucket list for her, do whatever we needed to in order to keep Kristi smiling.

We didn't even get a chance to put pen to paper.

Shortly after treatment began, Kristi started experiencing pain, nausea, and issues with ascites fluid buildup in her abdomen. This fluid is often produced as reaction to the presence of cancer in someone's abdomen, and can cause swelling, discomfort, nausea, and issues sleeping and eating. After numerous appointments to have the fluid drained, only to have it return a few days later, she was admitted to the hospital to find out exactly what was going on and why the fluid buildup was occurring so frequently.

Little did we know, this would be her last hospital visit. The hospital staff and the oncology team did everything in their power to make her comfortable as they ran tests. They drained the fluid from her belly, gave her medicine to reduce her nausea, and attempted to see if she could hold down food; but nothing seemed to work. Another CT scan was ordered, and it revealed that not only was the tumor in her hernia sac growing, but her stomach wall was now completely engulfed in cancer cells, and it was slowly killing her.

While everyone had been focused on the cancer in her hernia sac over the past few months, they didn't see how destructive this gradual thickening of her stomach wall was. The carcinomatosis had engulfed her stomach, making it impossible for her to eat, digest food, and gain nutrients. On Thursday, May 4th, with a room full of doctors, nurses, and healthcare professionals surrounding her, she was declared untreatable. There was nothing else Dr. Buttin and her staff could do to help my wife. They had been beaten. They could do nothing but look down, stare at their navels, and tell us how sorry they were and how much they loved my wife.

It's impossible to accurately describe the absolute shock we experienced in that moment. I don't know if I spoke a word of acknowledgement or not, but I know Jane, Kristi's friend, was so visibly upset with the news that she yelled at Dr. Buttin, questioning her prognosis, barely containing her fierce insistence that there must be something, anything they could do. Of course, there wasn't; but someone had to ask. I was paralyzed with shock. I couldn't speak, couldn't even form the words in my mind. Even if I could, nothing was going to change. We were told that the Northwestern Home Hospice Team would help us get Kristi home and prepare the house, so she could peacefully transition over the coming weeks surrounded by friends and family.

I was terrified. I had no idea know how incredibly difficult this was going to be. But I felt I could not show any weakness at the time. There would be time to cry and to fall apart when everything was over; this was not the day. Kristi needed my love, my compassion, and my care. She needed a hand to hold onto, and every ounce of strength I could muster. She needed me to be her husband.

The next three weeks are a blur. I was so focused on making sure that my wife was comfortable, that we did everything right, I'm not even sure how I came across to those around me. I drove her home that day devastated, knowing that no matter how hard I tried, no matter how hard I begged, there was nothing in the universe that was going to save my wife. I was literally driving her home to her death.

As I've mentioned before, I am a doer, not a nurturer. In my mind I saw my job as being the ultimate caregiver for my wife and making sure that at no point was she ever upset, in pain, uncomfortable, or nauseous. I did my best to understand how the various drugs worked, what kind of schedule we needed to keep her medications on. What we needed to do to keep her from being in pain, anxious, scared, alone. For the rest of her life, something which was to be counted in days and weeks, I just wanted her to feel loved.

Family members flew in, the house was prepared, and we did everything possible to make sure that she felt completely loved in these last days. Again, I don't know if I did a good job or not, but I tried. I tried with all my heart. I don't know if I was successful; I suppose I'll never know. But what I do know is this:

In these moments where life is defined in terms that you can measure, you cannot slow down, give up, or hand someone else the keys. You need to take charge, and you need to step up. There will be time for a rest when it's over, and there will be time to mourn when it's over, but when your wife is lying in bed dying, you need to make sure that everything is right. Was I devastated? Absolutely. Was I terrified? More than anyone will ever know. Was I prepared? Not in the least, but I moved forward and focused on her.

Three weeks can go past in the blink of an eye. Three weeks can be like a lifetime. The three weeks my wife was alive and in hospice at home were both, like being stuck in traffic while heading to a funeral. I will never forget how my wife fought to stay alive knowing she was going to die. How she joked and smiled at times despite knowing it was going to be over soon. How she struggled to stay involved in conversations with me and the other members of her family while drifting in and out of the necessary drug-induced haze, while her body slowly, and at times agonizingly, shut down. How she struggled with her own spirituality and was soothed by the words and kind voice of a minister sent to us by the Hospice Team. She whispered she loved me until she couldn't anymore, and she slipped away on the morning of May 25th as peacefully as she walked through this world.

The Journey: Scattering the Ashes

Kristi's death didn't "hit" me, in the way they talk about on television or in books. At least, not at first, and not all at once. Instead, I felt a haze descend upon me. Nothing seemed real or tangible; I was going through the motions. The simplest of tasks became Herculean in nature; the clearest of paths, now bewildering and at times illogical. Yet, as I waded in and out of the fog that enveloped me, I began to form a plan.

I wanted to do something more than simply place Kristi's ashes in an urn, or in a decorated box, to be placed on a shelf somewhere to gather dust. My wife's life was so full of love and warmth, which she shared indiscriminately with the people she loved. In death, I thought, her memory was best served by continuing that tradition.

And so, while planning her Celebration of Life and in the days following, I purchased small necklaces with pendants that could be filled with her ashes to give to her closest of friends and her family so that they would always have a small piece of Kristi close to them. Fifteen necklaces were purchased and handed out at her Celebration of Life, and the response from everyone was extremely gratifying. I also decided I would travel across the United States and Canada with small glass jars containing her ashes and spread them in all of the places we had loved, laughed, and shared memories with others.

The plan appeared simple at first, but it quickly became bigger than I had anticipated. I thought just a few locations would be enough; but, as I waded through our shared memories and experiences, I finally settled on twelve locations. Twelve places to share her with; twelve places which held some meaning both for her, and for the people in her life.

Little did I know, this act of sharing her would become one of the only reasons I'm convinced I survived her loss.

When a person dies, they leave people behind. It's easy, in the days, months, years that follow, to focus solely on the loss. The absence they leave in their wake. The fact is, the dead to not grieve; it's an experience shared only by the living, and only in sharing it do we find meaning.

We owned a travel trailer, which we had used to visit my stepson, to watch him play his college football games in Iowa. At first, I thought it would be the perfect way to travel the country and visit all the locations I planned to spread Kristi's ashes; but after looking at the map, and the distance I was going to travel, I quickly discovered this was not going to be the case. I traded the travel trailer in for a small, yet well-appointed 24-foot Winnebago View that would become my home for the next two months. And in July, I began packing things up and preparing for my trip.

Every stop was planned in advance. I put out the word to friends and family about my trip, and at that moment I was committed—as committed as I've ever been to anything in my life. I've always felt strongly that once you tell people you're going to do something, you cannot turn back. In fact, that's exactly how I quit smoking some eight years ago now.

My dog Jake, who would become the most amazing traveling companion, was my co-pilot. And I say co-pilot in every sense of the word. He grounded me, kept me going, and forced me to remember that I still had someone to care for, someone that needed me.

As the planning became more solid, more and more people began to ask when I expected to arrive at their location, and how long I was going to be there. I had never been on Facebook before, but I created a profile shortly after Kristi died so I could give myself a voice without hijacking her profile. While this outlet allowed me to reconnect with friends and family I hadn't talked to in years, even decades—what was more astounding to me was the fact that people who barely knew me, people who I never would have called close friends, quickly became the ones who were my greatest supporters, and insisted upon seeing me on my journey. This mission to spread Kristi's ashes was going to be much more than just a quiet, contemplative experience; it was quickly becoming a major life event.

On July 29th, Jake and I boarded the small RV, turned on the small Mercedes diesel engine of the Winnebago and headed west. I was nervous, I was excited, but there was also a sense of peace. I knew that what I was doing was exactly what Kristi wanted me to do. I was going to give her back to all the places we loved, the places *we* were loved, or that I believed deserved a piece of her.

Our first stop was Fort Collins, Colorado, which was two days' drive away. There's something about driving that is almost peaceful. The attention required doesn't allow you to be too distracted, but it does give you the ability to just *be,* to exist inside your own mind for a while. As we began heading west, I realized that what I was doing was extremely important. While I wouldn't quite grasp its magnitude until later, the tranquility I felt as I made my way cross country hinted at just how much I would get out of this trip in the days to come. It was something I needed to do.

As the day wore on and we wound our way through Iowa and into Nebraska, we finally settled in for the night at a small Campground eight hours from home. Setting up a small RV is fairly simple: you check-in, find your spot, park and level the unit, and then you go about connecting power, water, and your sewage line (if necessary). This entire process takes about 15 to 20 minutes if you know what you're doing. When Kristi and I would travel using our camper, the process usually took longer because there's just more to do with the bigger piece of equipment that's attached to a truck, versus something you're driving. The difference in experience, while seemingly insignificant, felt bittersweet. Before, she would be inside, handling the various tasks there, while I took care of what needed to be done outside. Of course, it wasn't that I minded taking on those tasks; but that with each step, I was reminded of everything I was missing.

Once set up, everything became about Jake. When you own a hyperactive miniature Australian Shepherd, you have to respect the fact that he needs attention, exercise, and a chance to explore. So, as would become the routine at every single campground, we went for a walk. Jake is no normal dog, and he has some challenges of his own. Walking him is sometimes a major task because he is so excited that he wants to meet and greet everyone, fend off other dogs from getting to close to his "daddy," and do so as quickly as possible. Often these "walks" were more like light jogs; but eventually he slowed down, did his business, and seemed to feel comfortable in his surroundings.

After our walk, and playing some games, we had a quick dinner and settled in for the evening. This was the first time in months that I truly felt alone without my wife. It was one of the most unsettling experiences I have ever had. With each task—gathering ingredients for dinner, preparing the meal, sitting down to eat, making up one half of the bed to sleep—each felt incomplete without her. She was truly gone. It was now, finally, that my mind was beginning to understand the gravity of what had happened. Naturally, the tears flowed, along with a few drinks to act as a sedative. As the evening grew dark, I slowly drifted off to sleep.

Day one was over. Only sixty-seven more to go.

Jake and I made our way to Fort Collins on the second day of our trip. We arrived early in the afternoon at a friend's place. The plan was to stay with Jim and Kathleen for a few days before heading west towards Sonoma,

California. This was the first time that I had to relive both the treatment and my wife's passing while explaining everything to someone else. Of course, none of this comes easy, but there was healing in telling her story. Especially when the story is about how much you love someone, the telling can be as cathartic as it is painful.

These were the early days of my grief, and every moment was raw. Jim and Kathleen made it easy for me, though. They have that Colorado way about them; calm, friendly, caring, and very good listeners. It was exactly what I needed to start this trip, and a beautiful example of the kind of support I would come to find nearly everywhere I went over the next two months.

Of course, no stay in Colorado is complete without several trips into the Hills, and with Jim as my guide I enjoyed some fantastic trail runs in the Colorado Foothills. These may have been the most cathartic runs of my entire life, and as a regular runner there have been many to compare. There's something about running in the wilderness that is both healing and soothing at the same time. And, while I don't know whether Kristi was there with me or not, I do believe that her energy was beside me with every panting breath Jake and I took.

Colorado was also the first place I would spread Kristi's ashes. Of the ten jars with me, the first was to be emptied high up in Rocky Mountain National Park. I don't think the day could have been any more perfect. The sun was bright, but the air was cool as it often is in the mountains. We drove with the windows down, and the trip up into Rocky Mountain Park was amazing as we crisscrossed the Big Thompson River, managed dozens of switchbacks, and stared at trees that seemed to defy gravity as they stretched into the sky. Jim, Jake, and I made it to the top of the park around midday, and found a good location, with the most incredible view of the Rockies and their natural majesty, to spread the first jar of ashes.

As I walked up a small pathway with tears in my eyes, I felt myself hesitate. It was all too real. It was all too final, and I wasn't truly ready; but ready or not, it didn't matter. This place was too beautiful not to go through with what I had planned. After finding a small spot with some privacy, with shaking hands and tear-stained cheeks I removed the cork from the bottle and proceeded to empty Kristi's ashes onto the lichen-covered field of the mountainside. I then took a brief moment to refill the jar with soil and moss to commemorate the location.

After placing the cork back in the bottle, I stopped, almost in shock or horror. At first, I wasn't sure what I had done. *Was this a bad idea?* A numbness came over me, and it felt as though the eyes of every selfie-seeking tourist were gawking at me; but as I lifted my head, all I could see was the expanse of the Rockies and their gift of beauty. Then, with tears streaming down my face, I gathered my senses and walked over to my friend. Not knowing what else to do, I gave him a quick, much-needed hug, and headed back towards the car. Jake was there waiting impatiently for us, and I let him out so he could enjoy the fresh air and the view for a few moments before we descended the mountain.

It was then that I realized having Jake with me in each of these moments was going to be crucial. He is my beautiful distraction: my energetic, and often overprotective four-legged anchor. He perched on a rock wall beside the road, and while I was worried he would fall off, or try and chase marmots, he sat down and smiled, a perfect head-tilted smile for me as if to say, "It's going to be okay, I've got you." This amazing dog, the last real gift Kristi ever gave me, would become my best friend and a source of healing and focus I can barely describe over the next eight weeks. In part, this story, and my future, is as much about him as it is about Kristi and me.

I was quiet on the way down the mountain. Partly, because I'm afraid of heights, and also because the real part of the journey had now begun. Giving Kristi back was, to me, as important as winning her over in the first place, but that is another story for another time. I felt as though it was my job to make sure that as many places as possible were gifted with a small piece of her.

On days like this, and moments like these, I felt the most at peace. I had given Kristi to the Rockies--a place she had never been, but always wanted to see. I felt fulfilled; I felt as though I was doing something right in a world where things aren't fair, where happy endings are not always the norm, and where life can sometimes end in the blink of an eye. Was I sad? Yes. But, there was a joy in this. A joy that I'll never forget, because she was with me the entire time.

"Life is full of grief, to exactly the degree we allow ourselves to love other people."
-Orson Scott Card, Ender's Shadow

"And so it has begun. I have taken you one last time, to somewhere you've never been, and left a small piece of you for Colorado to claim as its own. Kristi, you would have loved the views from here! They would have taken your breath away, and you would have held my hand, placed your head upon my shoulder, and felt the sunlight on your face as we sat in the cool mountain air. I can picture it now, all too clearly, behind tear-soaked eyes.

The beauty of The Rockies is only matched by yours. Tall, majestic, overwhelming at times, but also soft and subtle as you look closely at the moss and flowers covering the hills. Its rivers and streams remind me of our love; overflowing, turbulent, and yet calm where the eddies collect and the water rests before it continues its journey. The grasses sway in the wind as if dancing to a song yet unwritten, like you would do when no one was looking.

Take care of my wife, Colorado; she would have embraced you with all her heart."

Love,

H

And so it begins, Rocky Mountain National Park, CO.

Pit Stop: Finding Meaning

How did we get here?

Why her? Why me? Does anything matter? If so, which parts?

What will my life look like in this new world? Will I find love again quickly, or will I wait, wanting in misery, trying to figure out *everything* before doing *something*?

After Kristi's death, these questions and more battered my mind, leaving me aching for want of answers. I felt like a puzzle left unfinished, like so many of the pieces were missing I didn't even know which to look for. I scarcely knew which questions I'd answered, and which still lingered, like fog in low country before dawn fully breaks, clinging to the branches of trees yet to see the sun, knowing it will dissolve to return again tomorrow.

"The reality is that you will grieve forever. You will not 'get over' the loss of a loved one; you will learn to live with it. You will heal and you will rebuild yourself around the loss you have suffered. You will be whole again but you will never be the same. Nor should you be the same nor would you want to." -Kubler-Ross

As I waited for Kristi's Celebration of Life, I felt myself feeling as though I wasn't doing enough.

Finally, I decided that I needed to mark the event, and our life, permanently on my skin. I already had two tattoos about Kristi and her battle with cancer on my calves, so the idea seemed right. I designed a simple tattoo to be placed on my left forearm and had it completed. After looking down at the tattoo for a few days, it did not seem like enough, so I had another placed on my left shoulder just prior to the memorial. Despite the compliments and comments from friends and family, even these were not enough. Eventually, I had a total of eight added, and am now in the process of filling in the space between each of them. Whether these were enough or not, I've yet to figure out; but the world will know by looking at me that I was once truly in love with someone.

I believe a quiet hand was placed on my shoulder during this time, and it's still there now. I have yet to have a complete breakdown, but I know that one is always there looming on the horizon, potentially ready to drag me under with it. I have a volatile soul and a quiet anger that is always lurking deep down inside. My wife was the cure to that, and while there were times when she would become incredibly frustrated, she never once turned her back on me. It is this that I believe is keeping me from being pulled under. Whether it's the combination of memories or the photos and images I have of her, I get a sense of calm when I think about her. Sometimes this calm is accompanied with sadness, while at other times it brings me a sense of peace.

This was the kind of effect that she had not only on me, but on everyone around her. While I don't believe in angels, I do believe that my wife still has her eyes upon me, if eyes are the appropriate term. Maybe her energy is wrapped up in those memories. Maybe her soul isn't actually a soul at all, but the accumulation of all of the memories the world collectively has of her, creating an energy that is so great it cannot leave.

All I know is that I am still grounded. Even when I have had my darkest moments, and even when I have stared at the pistol on my nightstand and believed I would be better off with her, I have hesitated to act. I have hesitated to take the rash action that someone whose grief has become so unbearable takes in those moments. I have been able to step back and remember she loved me in spite of myself. She loved me when I didn't love myself. She loved me when I couldn't forgive myself. She loved me always. I can't say for certain why she did, but I believe it had something to do with my sense of loyalty to her and the fact that she knew I was there to take care of her through anything. I believe that was my role in life. I'm not sure what my role is now, but I have time to figure it out.

"The only way to end grief was to go through it."
— Holly Black, The Darkest Part of the Forest

The Journey: Shadow Boxing

My emotions were running particularly high, and I knew it was time to move on. So that evening I prepared the RV for departure. After a wonderful dinner, I gave a small pair of earrings to Kathleen from the bins of Kristi's jewelry I had with me, and we headed to bed. Jake and I said our goodbyes in the morning and headed west towards California. Spending four wonderful days with Jim and Kathleen was the perfect start to this trip. I knew there would be more introspective and, quite possibly, dark times ahead; but at that moment, as I was heading towards Utah, I was glad to have had the opportunity to share my odyssey with them.

Our next destination was Grass Valley, California, home of a former coworker and friend, John, his wife Uta, and their son Max. I arrived at mid-afternoon and very quickly introduced Jake to Max and the other dogs. Jake and Max became instant friends as Jake showed off some of his better tricks and agility moves, but I'm not so sure the other dogs appreciated the intrusion. That evening the four of us went into town for a quiet dinner, and afterwards John and I stayed out to explore a little bit of the town.

Grass Valley is an eclectic mix of hippies and well-to-do's, and is essentially a mosaic of California culture. The town is small, yet bustling at night, and has a distinct vibe or aura about it; one you could almost call a drum beat that pulses outward from the bars and restaurants. It is exactly the kind of place Kristi and I would have loved spending a weekend. We spent a couple hours bar hopping and mingling with the locals, before exhaustion got the better of me and it was time to call it a night. Looking back on that evening, I believe it was one of the first times since Kristi died that I didn't secretly dread going back to the RV and to bed.

I had originally planned to spend only one evening with John and Uta, but that idea was quickly dispelled when they invited me to spend the following day with them on the water in one of the nearby lakes. I had made better time that I expected crossing Utah and Nevada, and now had an extra day in my schedule, so after what can only be described as token arm twisting, I decided to join them. The next morning, Uta made sandwiches, raided the pantry and fridge, and, with Jake in tow, we headed towards one of the local marinas.

I had purchased Jake a life jacket for the trip, and the moment he put it on I could tell he was excited. As we worked our way down the lake in a rented speedboat, I could sense that my dog was indeed a water dog. Jake is a miniature Australian Shepherd, a herding dog, so this was not something I had expected, nor did I ever imagine how happy it would make me to see him running around in and out of the water for hours. We spent the entire day on the lake moving between a couple of different beaches, playing on a tow-behind tube we had in the boat with us, and enjoying the sun. John was our skipper, Max and Jake were our entertainment, and Uta and I enjoyed watching the day unfold while sipping beers and enjoying the sandwiches.

Later that evening, after we arrived back at the house, I brought out two small bins of Kristi's jewelry and sat down with Uta. Even though she did not know Kristi, and would never have the opportunity to meet her, she immediately accepted my offer and chose a couple of timeless pieces of jewelry that she promised she would wear at an upcoming event. Uta also told me about her loss in recent years, and how she too was searching for answers in a world where they're not handed out easily. Her father had passed away, and she had taken a trip to find peace as well. Like me, she was still looking. I believe the sharing of our stories, the connection we made, will last us a lifetime.

"The most beautiful people we have known are those who have known defeat, known suffering, known struggle, known loss, and have found their way out of

the depths. These persons have an appreciation, a sensitivity, and an understanding of life that fills them with compassion, gentleness, and a deep loving concern. Beautiful people do not just happen." -Kubler-Ross

---

The drive from Grass Valley to Sonoma, California on a Sunday can be a little hectic, and even though I've driven hundreds of thousands of miles in my life, I am not a fan of going downhill or being in busy traffic, especially while driving a 25" RV that, at times, can seem a little wobbly. Despite the stress of driving downhill for what seemed like forever, we made our way to the Russian River Valley in great time, and we were comfortably situated at our riverside campsite by mid-afternoon.

Sonoma is one of the places where Kristi and I had enjoyed a fantastic vacation together years ago. Being back here stirred memories I had thought long forgotten. The wine tours, wonderful dinners, walking around in downtown Sonoma, the fantastic Fairmont resort we stayed in, were all part of the painting in my head. Just being in wine country was emotional, but being alone brought with it a sense of finality. This wasn't the anniversary vacation we had shared before; this was a mission.

Thankfully, some old friends from another time in my life, Erin and Ray, took the time out of their week to drive up from San Jose and meet me. They were staying the night at a nearby hotel and planned to accompany me the following day on a short winery tour. Specifically, the Gary Farrell Winery, where I planned to spread the second jar of Kristi's ashes. They arrived late in the afternoon, and after extended hugs and some initial tears, we sat for hours reminiscing and catching up like only old friends can. I hated the fact that I was using my wife's death as an opportunity to reconnect with old friends; but at the same time, I was glad they were with me. There had to be good things to come out of her passing, and this was one of them.

There's something comforting about sitting around a fire with old friends that just cannot be replicated. The light scent of burning firewood. The soothing symphony of crickets and frogs in the background, punctuated now and again by the hoot of an owl, the call of a coyote in the distance, or the light, bubbling sound of laughter at a well-told joke. This was something Kristi and I would do often at our house, or when camping with our travel trailer. I designed our backyard to be a place where everyone was welcome, day or night. In the evening you had the choice of sitting down by the fire pit, hanging around the outdoor kitchen, or sitting in front of the fireplace. Most times, we chose the fire pit. There's something more rustic, more connected with nature about it. That Sunday night with Ray and Erin was exactly the kind of night Kristi and I would have loved. Sitting around telling stories, drinking wine, and making the kinds of connections that can only occur in those perfect twilight evenings, when no one has to be up early, every care and burden of the day set aside to ease the ache in the shoulders, and the soul. I wish she had been there with us. Maybe she was.

"We bereaved are not alone. We belong to the largest company in all the world--the company of those who have known suffering."
— Helen Keller, We Bereaved

The following day was a big one for us. Our first stop was a winery that Erin and Ray had been to before, and after arriving and hanging out for a little bit they allowed Jake to come into the Tasting Room. As usual Jake was the hit of the day, and the people at the winery fell in love with him as he did his best imitation of an Australian Shepherd desperately trying to control his uncontrollable self even though his wiggling butt gave him away. Thankfully the wine was also delicious, so we spent a good hour and a half here before heading up to the Gary Farrell Vineyards.

The Gary Farrell Vineyards held a special place in our hearts. Kristi and I fell in love with their wines in the early 2000's, had visited the winery in 2007 to celebrate our 5th Anniversary, and we had hoped to get back sometime in the near future. Of course, now we were visiting for another reason.

The staff at the winery was unbelievably accommodating, and they allowed me to bring Jake through their dining room and out onto the main patio. Now, Jake is not the kind of dog you can "take through" anywhere. He is so full of energy that almost everything is a distraction, so instead of having him bumble through the dining room, pulling on his leash with the strength of a much larger dog, I picked him up by his backpack handle and carried him through the dining room, feet dangling, ears back, staring at people with his one blue eye and one brown eye, begging them to look away and not laugh.

On the patio we proceeded to take a few photos of the amazing hills and views of the surrounding Russian River Valley before I stepped onto the grassy hillside to spread Kristi's ashes. It's an odd feeling when you're doing something that's incredibly painful, yet also unbelievably fulfilling. Here I was, with two old friends and my dog, spreading Kristi's ashes onto the mountainside of our favorite winery. I sadly realized, through tear filled eyes, that I would never be back here again with her; yet, I was oh so glad of the memories we had created some ten years ago. Were it not for those memories, this entire trip would be meaningless, after all.

Morning haze at the Gary Farrell Winery, Russian River Valley, CA.

But tears don't last forever, and when you're surrounded by people who love you, they do their best to bring you back to where you belong. That is just what Erin and Ray did. We sat there for another half hour or so sipping wine, talking, and simply enjoying the view from their incredible patio. Jake, of course, was doing his best imitation of a dog that doesn't get enough attention, but all in all was well-behaved. I truly believe he had a sense of when he needed to be calm, and when he was allowed to be his normal mischievous, occasionally crazy self. He just seemed to have an intuition for that. After we finished our tasting and I purchased a few bottles of wine, we loaded ourselves into the car once more and headed towards another opportunity to talk about Kristi and what life was like with her while enjoying the taste of some of the Russian River Valley's finest.

I don't know if I can ever thank Erin and Ray for how much they helped me that day. Not only was it unbelievably emotional and something I probably could not have done alone, but I felt I was somehow saying goodbye. Saying goodbye to the opportunity to sit once again in the beautiful Russian River Valley with my wife, enjoying an amazing glass of wine and her smile in the California sun.

The following day I had completely to myself. It was just Jake and I hanging out at the campground, enjoying the beautiful weather and spending time at the Russian River. This is what I called a "down day" on the trip, a day simply to get a few things done and taken care of before heading to the next stop. And the next stop was a full day's drive away, in San Diego, California. Jake and I spent the day relaxing, doing some laundry, and generally just taking it easy. The emotional toll the day before had taken on me needed to be respected, and I was glad to have a day of quiet and rest before our early start the next morning.

The drive to San Diego was a long, hot fourteen hours, but uneventful. Kristi and I had been here numerous times, and it was one of the places we had considered moving to in a few years, when the boys were finished with college and well-established in their new jobs. If any place deserved to share some of Kristi, this was it. The question was where I should spread her ashes.

After looking online, the logical choice jumped out at me - Ocean Beach. There's an off leash dog beach right next door which would give Jake the opportunity to experience the ocean, maybe play with other dogs (something he doesn't really do) and get a feel for what it was like to jump around in the surf.

I packed up our things, grabbed an Uber from our KOA into the city, and after making sure Jake was "dog friendly," we spent hours at the beach, and he loved every minute of it. After play time, I took the small jar and walked over to the large pier. I found a quiet spot away from everyone to spread Kristi's ashes into the ocean. Emotion washed over me in time with the waves, strong, steady, unrelenting. There was a sense of accomplishment, a sense of sorrow, and a sense of joy as I watched the ashes settle along the damp rocks, to be washed away by each splash of ocean spray.

Ocean Beach, San Diego, CA.

I can't say I left Ocean Beach happy, but I can say I left Ocean Beach satisfied. And as the waves beat their steady tempo against the rocks, I was able to walk away once again with tears in my eyes and a love song pounding in my heart.

The real lesson of the hill is that when you think you have reached your limit, you are underestimating yourself. - Jonathan Grayson

---

At this point in the journey, the reality of my situation was starting to set in. I was alone with my four-legged companion, seven remaining jars of ashes, and approximately eight thousand miles of road stretching out before me. I had already driven 1/3 of the trip, but this was the easy part. The next few destinations were filled with Kristi's friends and family and were sure to be more emotional.

As expected, the following day, as I was heading towards Arizona, I was hit with a wave of emotion. People had been reaching out to me now for months, and I was becoming aware of how certain people made it a point to contact me, while others, who I had assumed would take a larger role, slid into the background. For example, one of Kristi's relatives, who couldn't make the two-and-a-half-hour drive from Los Angeles to San Diego to see me and get the gifts I had for her, the day after I had driven 14 hours by myself. I called this the "popping up and popping down" effect, much like a game of whack-a-mole, where certain people popped up to check in on me and others popped down or simply slipped away and disappeared. Over the course of the trip, the people who I had envisioned being my greatest supporters were not the ones who popped up; largely, it was people I hadn't talked to in years; family, old friends, former co-workers, etc. who were reaching out in droves.

Maybe it's the sense of family that growing up in a small town brings, or maybe it's just a difference in culture. It could also be that my true friends and family were a lot further away than I had thought. My life in Illinois had been defined in every way by Kristi, and most of my friends there were connected to me through her. As such, I became painfully aware that when I got home in early October, it wouldn't be home anymore. This was something I was not only dreading, but deep down, I was beginning to doubt I'd still fit in when all of this was over.

Still, I was looking forward to getting to Arizona. A friend of Kristi's was diagnosed with ovarian cancer around a year after she was, and unbeknownst to Kristi, her oncologist asked if the friend would be willing to talk to "someone" about her treatment. We had no idea who this person was, other than the fact that her name was Gail, and that she would be contacting Kristi. Of course, you never think the world is as small as it is until you find out just how interconnected we all are. Kristi received a call and a voice message from a lady named Gail, and was surprised to find out, when she returned the call, that she was a longtime friend from work.

Immediately upon reconnecting, the two of them began to share stories and concerns about how their treatment was going, and exactly how life would unfold for them and their families. I don't know the extent of all their conversations, but I've been told that they were many. Often tearful, sometimes afraid, but always filled with love and support. This is what cancer does; while it's ripping lives and families apart, it also brings people together, not knowing for how long or for what purpose, in many instances, until it's all over. I know Gail's husband, Steve, and I are very similar, and as doers, we did our very best to support them both during their treatments. I know Steve continues to do so today, as Gail continues to fight her own war against this terrible disease.

When I arrived in Phoenix, just seeing Gail made my heart ache. She looked healthy, but frail, and wore the smile of a cancer survivor: the kind of reserved smile that appreciates life, understands sorrow, and even deeper down, understands that time is limited, and therefore makes the very best of it. At the same time, she was also sad; sad for my loss, sad for the loss of her friend, and for the knowledge that this disease may someday sneak up on her; something I truly hope never happens.

We talked about my trip and shared a few memories, and then quickly tried to make my visit into something that wasn't so much focused on Kristi's death, but about old friends connecting over a common bond. After getting a good night of sleep, the next morning we went hiking in the Arizona desert, where Jake was the victim of some nasty burs and the hot Arizona sun. Like a trooper he handled both without complaint, but needless to say we will not be moving to Arizona any time soon. That night, we had a great BBQ dinner at a local restaurant that smelled of wood chips and mesquite, and enjoyed a few drinks and laughs. It was exactly what I had hoped it would be; a chance to reconnect, share, and be together surrounded by our love of an amazing woman, my Kristi. I do recall Gail trying to steal Jake from me at one point, but neither he nor I were having anything to do with it—sorry Gail!

As I continued my journey East towards Texas, the next few days allowed me to simply lose myself in solitude. I traveled up to Sedona and spent a quiet evening just outside of town. I enjoyed the desert heat in the evening, and the breeze coming through the camper. I thought a lot about what life would hold for me, and just how torn I was that I didn't get to share it with Kristi anymore. I spent time with Jake, and as our bond continued to grow, the love I had for that dog seemed to have no bounds. We travelled to places like Las Cruces, New Mexico, where Billy the Kid once hid from the law, and Tombstone, Arizona, the location of the famous gunfight at the OK Corral, stopping, taking little walking tours to stretch our legs, posing for goofy photos and getting some fresh air when possible, then made our way across Texas to San Antonio.

I was really looking forward to getting to San Antonio. I needed to stop in and reconnect with an old business friend that I've known for years. Don is one of these people that, immediately upon meeting him, I knew we were going to be friends. He had a great industry track record, a personality somewhat like mine, and faces life and its challenges head on. His advice and candid conversation were sorely needed on this trip. It was one of those things that I just felt I had to do. He also knew Kristi and was able to make that small connection I needed to ensure that I wasn't going insane, reassuring me, at a crucial time, that what I was doing really did have value.

Jake doing his best imitation of an outlaw in Sedona, AZ.

He, his wife Carla, and I had a quiet dinner that night. We talked of life and love and enjoyed each other's company. We talked about Kristi and our relationship, how much I missed her. While at times the tears were mere inches away, I managed to make it through dinner without completely breaking down. I feel that every single conversation like this has value. As painful as they may be, there are insights to be gained every single time you talk about the person you've lost. It might be a memory you'd forgotten, or a small detail that comes back to you in a flash; but these conversations hold so much value that you have to get through them, even if getting through them feels like pouring salt into an open wound.

Grief is an invisible, intangible enemy. The more you try to fight it, the more you end up hurting yourself.

Pit Stop: Remembering

Memories are the thoughts, feelings and emotions we attach to a person, a place, or a special time in our lives. They're deeply personal, and wholly owned by you. No one can change them; they cannot be taken away or stolen from you, no matter how hard someone else tries.

I believe memories of loved ones aren't designed to make us sad, but to make us happy. Over time the memories that remain with us are the ones we go back to the most. They bring us closer to that person, place, and time than anything else, so we "visit" with them more often. They become a huge part of who we are and how we remember someone. They are our "comfort food" when we think of that person taking us back to a special event or feeling, allowing us to be with them whenever we want.

I have some amazing memories of Kristi that will never fade away.

Some of them are funny, like karaoke and dancing on the back patio the night of her 50th birthday party. She was a self-admitted terrible singer, but she stood up and gave it her all that night, throwing herself into every song. We all had a good laugh and too many drinks, but inside, I felt that her voice was the most beautiful thing I'd ever heard, because it was uniquely her: genuine, and full of life.

Some memories are romantic or peaceful, like our 10th Anniversary in Hawaii. One day we sat on the rocks drinking white wine, watching the kite boarders with their multi-colored sails tame the wind and waves. There were people everywhere, but it felt as if we were alone.

Then there were the simple moments as we enjoyed our morning coffee— mine with cream and sugar, and hers with just cream—then fruit and a bagel at this little restaurant across from the Paia Hotel. Or sitting under the trees and staring off at the ocean sunset without a care in the world before heading to Mama's for dinner. Holding hands as the sun sank into the ocean, and silently asking ourselves how we got so lucky.

I sometimes wonder if Kristi and I would have travelled extensively again. I am sure we would have, and we would have loved every minute of it: the planning, the wait in the airport lounge before boarding our flight, the rolled eyes and look of exasperation as I laughed at her while ordering "one last drink," and the intimate moments that require no explanation at all when you're with the person you love.

Of course, there are sad memories; no loss happens without sadness, but I consciously choose not to focus on those. I remember her the way I want to: my beautiful, funny, caring, kind, intelligent wife who had that little bit of spice when she needed it.

As I immerse myself in memories, I've discovered that I need to get comfortable with the idea that grief and mourning are not just pathways, they are more like rivers. They flow continually and without any consciousness or care for time or their surroundings. There are moments when the current is slow and the water calmly makes its way downstream, there are times when the current is quick, overpowering and unforgiving and there are times when I feel like I am slowly drowning in a deep pool of sadness and uncertainty.

One of the many amazing sunsets in Maui, Oct 2012.

For the past few weeks it has seemed as though I could barely sense the water flowing past my ankles. Like a hot day late in August when the water is low and the sand bars are high, I have felt at ease. I have been standing in a stream of grief, but it was palatable; surging only at moments when certain songs are played on the radio or when something familiar strikes me or catches my eye. Maybe it's the winter? Maybe my mourning has frozen like so many lakes and rivers, silently waiting to thaw in spring and reawaken my mind to the loss that has upended me and cast me adrift? I am not sure, but all that ended today, 40 days before spring.

It's raining today and somewhere a river is swelling up, it's banks heaving, muddy water ready to engulf me and take me under. I won't let it of course. I'll step back from the bank and watch it flow by, gazing in awe of its power to give and take away, while I listen to its story and learn from its meaning. In the meantime, I will continue to miss the gentle wake you left behind as you walked through life beside me.

I woke up this morning and thought of you. I rolled to my left to see if you were there and of course you weren't. It's been months now since you've been gone, your voice an echo in the darkness of the morning. Were you a ghost all those years? I told your spirit I missed you and then I lay there wondering what I will make of my life in the end. Will I have my own story to tell? I had it all planned out before May 25th, now I am still searching for something to grab onto and make my own. I struggle to find meaning, reason, purpose or the ability to love myself like you loved me. I need time...seasons.

Shortly before what would have been her 52nd birthday, I was going through some of her things, and came across a collection of greeting cards for all kinds of occasions. I don't know who most of these cards were purchased for, or if they were even purchased with anyone in mind; but I can picture my wife strolling down the aisle of Walgreens or Target fingering through cards, smiling and laughing to herself in a way that only she could. I am certain she thought about her friends and the relationships she valued every day of her life; it's just who she was.

While I don't own how Kristi is remembered by anyone else, I do own how she is remembered by me. Not a day goes by where I don't look at her picture and that incredible smile. And it makes me happy, because life is too short to stay sad.

For those of you who have lost someone, I know you have your favorite memories, and I hope you find as much comfort in yours as I do. For even if they bring tears to your eyes in the moment, the happiness that follows is worth the pain.

"...we are all sorry when loss comes for us. The test of our character comes not in how many tears we shed but

in how we act after those tears have dried." — Michelle Moran, *Madame Tussaud: A Novel of the French Revolution*

The next day I headed over to the other side of the city to see Kristi's nieces. Kristi has two nieces, Tayler and McKenzie that have been close to her ever since they were born. One played a vitally important role during Kristi's final days in home hospice. Tayler was simply amazing. For a young woman of only 24 years, she showed the grace and courage of someone much older and wiser. I had never envisioned her this way, but after seeing her care for my wife, helping me prepare and deliver her medications, assisting the hospice nurses, bathing, and ensuring Kristi was completely comfortable at all times, I cannot express how much I appreciate everything she did. All she wanted to do was care for Kristi, and she did it so tremendously well. Unfortunately, she wasn't able to be there by her side when Kristi passed away, but she was there for her Celebration of Life, and I know that at some point during the ceremony her Aunt reached down, put a hand on her shoulder and whispered in her ear, "I love you. Thank you, Tayler."

Visiting the girls was fun, and over the course of a weekend we enjoyed each other's company, some great food, many drinks, and dozens of memories and laughs. Jake got along with the resident dog for the most part, only terrorizing her once, and the girls managed to put up with their step-Uncle invading their space. As Sunday rolled around Kristi's sister Kelly, and one of Kristi's closest friends from Illinois, Julie, arrived at the girls' house. We went out for dinner that evening, and after arriving back home we once again opened the bins with Kristi's remaining jewelry. The girls were given the opportunity to go through everything one last time (they had already done so at the Celebration of Life) and take any last pieces that they wanted for themselves. Sometimes, all we have is the physical, and holding on to these things can be extremely important. I didn't want the want the girls to lose the opportunity to have these small remnants of her.

Before the trip, I had also made Shadow Boxes for several people, with Julie's help, using some of Kristi's jewelry. So it was great to have Julie there when I gave each of them their customized shadow boxes. Kelly, Tayler, and McKenzie received their shadow boxes that night, and I was very proud to know this little part of someone that was so special in their lives will be with them forever. I don't know whether I was doing this for her, or if I was doing it for me, but I had the overwhelming feeling that I was giving as much of Kristi back to the world as she gave to it, and to me.

The next day all the girls and I traveled up to the small town of Concan, Texas, where the Frio River runs through. We had vacationed here with Kristi's family on several occasions over the past few years and had truly enjoyed the experience. We made our way to a section of the river where the five of us could relax and enjoy the sunshine before spreading the fourth jar of Kristi's ashes. Jake played in the water, chasing after one of his many soccer balls, while we sat around taking everything in. After a short while, the four girls took small handfuls of Kristi's ashes and released them into the Frio River. She was now a part of Texas, just like she was a part of the Rockies, Pacific Ocean, and the Russian River Valley. Almost immediately after releasing the ashes into the river, out of nowhere a rainbow appeared. I don't know if the rainbow meant anything or if it was a blessing from Kristi, but it was enough to be noticed, and everyone appreciated it for that.

"No matter how bad your heart is broken, the world doesn't stop for your grief."— Faraaz Kazi

---

The soothing Frio River, Concan, TX.

My time in Texas wasn't over, but it was time to leave San Antonio and head down to South Padre Island, where Kelly and her husband Dan call home. Over the past few years, Kristi, realizing that her time on earth was limited, had visited them on numerous occasions. Even though I had only visited once, I thought it was appropriate to spend a little time there and spread some of her ashes in the bay near their home. Despite a tropical storm heading straight towards the island, Kelly, Julie, and Tayler drove down to the island in separate vehicles, while Jake and I trailed behind in the RV. The next evening, we had the opportunity, on a beautifully calm night, to sit on the pier and release more fragments of my darling into the waters of the Gulf of Mexico.

I was beginning to notice, during the ash spreading ceremonies, that a pattern was developing. Each time I released them I was becoming more and more calm, my emotions less intense, easier to bear, and I was adjusting to the idea that these weren't so much funerals as births. It felt as though I was giving something to the world, rather than taking something from it, and I think that was extremely important for me during this process. Jake's demeanor also continued to change whenever we were doing them, as if he knew the importance each time. Maybe when Kristi passed a small bit of her energy became a part of him, or maybe he just sensed how important it was; I'll never know. But at moments it seemed as though these ceremonies were as significant to him as they were to me.

Perhaps the easing of my own tension and emotions fueled the looming storm's fury. The next day Tropical Storm Harvey became Hurricane Harvey, and after finishing a load of laundry and running out to get the third tattoo (a compass with an arrow through it) added to my left arm, I had to quickly gather up our belongings, load the RV and head north to avoid any potential issues from the pending storm.

Sunset on South Padre Island, TX.

Jake and I drove from South Padre Island to New Braunfels, Texas, and spent a quiet evening in a small campground that night. The following morning, after a cup of coffee and some breakfast, I had a phone session with my long-time therapist and life coach, Nick, and it was then that I realized the toll that the trip was taking on me. I believe I cried for almost the entire 50 minutes while talking to him. I was emotionally exhausted, and it was beginning to show. I had been so busy the past two and a half months, I don't know if I had taken the time to truly miss my wife; but it was that morning I realized how much I missed her, how much it hurt knowing I would never see her again, and that for all intents and purposes, I was alone.

Like all storms, grief is meant to end. As you emerge out the other side you will be at peace, surrounded by the people who truly love you, having shed those who don't. Take your time. It's a path, and wherever you are right now is exactly where you're supposed to be.

In order to avoid the hurricane, I travelled North to Dallas. I had previously arranged to meet a friend of mine from Florida, in Houston. Tim was planning to travel with me for the trip from Houston over to Florida to keep me company and break up the boredom of driving alone. Given the weather, he instead flew into Dallas and met up with me that evening. After Jake checked him out thoroughly to make sure he was allowed to be in the RV, we sat around that night and talked about my wife, the trip, Jake, and what the future might hold. I don't know if we solved any of the world's problems, but between the red wine and some of Kristi's left over medical THC edibles, we may have come up with a few ideas and planted a few seeds.

It was good to have someone traveling with me. Up until this point I had driven the entire way by myself, with only Jake as a co-pilot/navigator. And, unfortunately, he's unable to speak, and likes to sneak off into the back of the RV after we get moving. Tim, on the other hand, has no mute button, and from Dallas all the way to Orlando, we talked about everything. It was good to have someone in the RV with me. It makes the drive much easier, and it's always better to have someone to communicate with rather than allowing negative thoughts to rattle around inside of your own head.

After shaking off our minor hangovers, the following morning we headed Southeast across Texas and Mississippi to Pensacola, Florida with plans to meet up with a friend of his that night and watch the widely televised Mayweather vs. McGregor boxing match. We went out that night and enjoyed ourselves while watching the fight on the lawn of a local bar. It wasn't the best place to watch a boxing match, or have a few drinks for that matter, but it was good to be out in the real world rather than sitting in the RV for the 3rd night in a row.

The next morning, Tim, Jake and I packed up the RV and spent a few hours at the National Naval Aviation Museum looking at planes and taking photos before we ventured over to the beach for a short visit. After some fun in the waves on the beach with Jake, who is obsessed with catching balls, we continued our travels east to Tallahassee, and then from Tallahassee to Orlando. We made good time on both days, and I dropped Tim off at the Orlando Airport around noon, knowing I would see him and some other friends again in a few days on my way North from Florida to Eastern Canada.

From there Jake and I headed south to Naples, Florida, where Kristi's parents called home. I wasn't dreading the thought of seeing her parents, but I was nervous. These were the people who raised her, the ones that helped make her the person she was; the person I loved, and the person I missed so much. In the back of my mind I think I was always a little worried whether I was a good enough husband, a good enough stepfather, and a good enough son-in-law. I am my harshest critic, and were it not for Kristi's constant reminders that I was good enough, I'm not sure whether or not the demons in my head would have been held a bay or gotten the better of me.

Catching some air in Pensacola before the drive to Naples, FL.

As it turned out, I had nothing to worry about. Kristi's parents welcomed me with open arms. It was good to be with them. We had talked on numerous occasions during the trip, but of course, seeing someone in person always gives you a better sense of how they're doing. Kristi's mother, who is a battle-hardened cancer survivor, treated me like the son she never had, and her father Jim, who I know took Kristi's passing very hard, was wonderful. For the next two and a half days we spent our time hanging out, watching movies, playing with Jake in the pool, and enjoying each other's company.

On my last night with them we went to dinner, and I don't know what sparked it, but we began to talk about Kristi. It was then I realized I was never going to stop missing her. That she would always be with me in some small way. While trying to hold back the tears at dinner, I think we all realized that the grieving was never going to stop; the loss will always linger with us, and will be a part of everything we do moving forward. But I think we also realized that it's okay. That grief can transform into something soothing and comforting. Like a butterfly emerging from its cocoon, all those memories that make you sad will eventually put a smile on your face and lift your heart. Of course, I was still a long way off from that, but with each passing day, and each conversation, the journey towards acceptance would occur.

On the morning before I left we took the jar of Kristi's ashes and, rather than placing them in the ocean, we decided to spread them in amongst the soil of their backyard. During our numerous trips to Florida over the years, her parents' backyard and pool was where we spent most of our time, and made the most memories, so it seemed most appropriate that we place her remains there. I was also able to give a shadow box to Linda, so she would have another reminder of the daughter she had lost, but will always love and carry in her heart.

"Grief can be a burden, but also an anchor. You get used to the weight, how it holds you in place."
— Sarah Dessen, The Truth About Forever

She will always be close by you, Naples, FL.

Leaving my in-laws was bittersweet, but I needed to keep moving. I had a schedule set in my mind, and I didn't want to linger any longer. If I sit still for too long, I think on things to the point of obsession. I get restless, even if I just try to sit calmly in a space. I think I was meant to be in motion; that might be, in part, why the trip was so good for me.

I needed a break from the ashes, however, and the proximity to Kristi's death everything else was bringing me. So, I travelled over to Melbourne, Florida, where I have several friends from a company I used to work for years ago. Jake and I spent the weekend in Melbourne Beach with Gene and Val, enjoying each other's company, talking about the future, and even the possibility of moving down to Florida if I sold my home in Illinois and decided to make a move to someplace new. It was all very fascinating, and very real, but a part of me didn't really think it was practical. Gene and I talked about the job market along the Space Coast and some possibilities there, or maybe doing something completely different like opening a coffee shop where people can hang out, enjoy good coffee, good company, and great Wi-Fi. I even have a name for this coffee shop: Island Grind. Maybe someday I'll own that little coffee shop. For the moment, though, there was a road to travel between me and the dream.

After two great days with Gene and Val, I spent my last night at Tim's place, catching up with him some more and helping his daughter Erin celebrate her 18th birthday, before I began my trip north towards Charleston, SC. Charleston was another one of the cities Kristi and I had considered moving to within the next couple years. We spent a weekend there a few years ago and had truly enjoyed everything about the city. I like old places; I believe they have a soul, and that their history creates not only a sense of the past, but a vision of their future. Charleston is the quintessential old American city, as its history echoes in the architecture and the stories that are told about it. Stories of pirates like Blackbeard, of naval battles and blockades, and all of those things that children's tales are made of. At the same time, it's a bustling city full of opportunity.

I arrived in Charleston late in the afternoon. It was a nice day, but too hot for a run, so I opted to stay near the camper, go for a walk, and play with Jake a little bit in the dog run they had on site. Jake only has two speeds: Stop and Go. So, for a good fifteen minutes he was in full Go mode, and by the end of it, in the Charleston heat and humidity, he was exhausted and ready for a nice cool nap in the RV.

We spent a quiet night in the small RV park south of Charleston, and I began planning where I would take Kristi's ashes and spread them in the morning. The next day we drove to a public beach Northeast of Charleston. Jake and I walked down to the beach, which was teeming with people, because it was almost noon by the time we arrived. We walked out into the water, and after clumsily removing the cork from the bottle, I poured Kristi's ashes into the ocean.

The moment I saw them falling into the water I knew something wasn't quite right—but it was too late. As I scrambled to identify the source of my unease, I realized that I had convinced myself Kristi's ashes needed to be spread near water. In retrospect, this was not the case.

Her ashes needed to be spread where it had meaning to me, and a connection to her. Somehow, I had lost my way. Jake and I stood on the beach for a moment as I contemplated my mistake, then we hurriedly walked back to the RV to begin heading north again, regret streaming from the corners of my eyes.

I now know where the ashes should have been spread. In fact, I have two choices. The first is an old plantation we visited during that weekend vacation to Charleston in 2010, and the second is the abandoned lighthouse that sits off the shore of Charleston we also visited on that same trip. Someday, I'll get over there and correct my mistake, but for now, like with all of my errors in life, I will simply have to accept it and move forward.

On my way north, an old friend of Kristi's contacted me and asked if I could travel to Greenville, North Carolina, to see them. Although not originally on my plan, as I had hoped to travel away from the Atlantic coast to I-81, and then North to Connecticut, I felt it was the right thing to do.

I arrived at their house late in the afternoon, somewhat tired after a long day, but glad to see Jackie and Dave because I hadn't seen them in years. Kristi and Jackie had grown apart after Jackie had moved away, but in the past few years, the two of them had reconnected after Jackie discovered Kristi was diagnosed with cancer. Since reconnecting they had sent countless messages and notes to one another, unbeknownst to me, and I was glad to hear of this when I sat down with them for dinner. We spent the night enjoying a great meal, reminiscing and talking about Kristi as if she were just one room away. She did feel close as I reconnected with her friend. I again took out the box with Kristi's remaining jewelry, and Jackie was more than happy to take several pieces I know she will wear with pride.

The side trip was short but sweet, and the next morning I resumed my path north. As with many of the nights sleeping in the RV, I was very melancholy the next day. Despite the fact that I had a great traveling companion in Jake, he simply couldn't talk, and although he provided me joy in so many ways, he wasn't able to put a hand on mine, or provide me a shoulder to lean on when I was feeling particularly lonely.

It's interesting how much value we place on human companionship, or in fact, how little *conscious* value we place on it. We take for granted the little things that our spouses and companions do, like purchasing a gift as they pass by something they think we'd love, or leave us notes when they go 't, or ask us how our day was. Any of the thousands of things people do when they're part of a couple. This was something I was really beginning to miss, and it wasn't the first time I'd noticed it, miles and miles to go with Jake in the back of the RV and nobody in the seat beside me.

I spent a quick night in Connecticut at a former colleague and friend of mine's house, Tom. We enjoyed a quiet dinner at a trendy Mexican restaurant while his wife Amy was out with friends, and in the morning, I made my way North towards Bangor, Maine. Unfortunately, the drive was interrupted by a pit stop at a Mercedes dealership in Massachusetts to replace a battery that had failed. The stop was brief, Jake kept the service team entertained with his soccer dribbling skills, and in no time, we were back on the road, and made it through Massachusetts without the typical Boston traffic slowing us down. As the day wore on, it began to rain, and by the time I arrived at the campsite in Maine, I was tired. The trip was taking its toll on me, and that night, as the rain softly fell on the roof of the RV, I felt the weight of that loneliness, which I'd managed to hide from for a while, creeping in to wrap cold fingers around my heart.

The next day, I crossed the Canadian border and made my way to see an old friend I hadn't talked to in over 20 years. She was in fact my first crush, my elementary school love, if childhood romance and my awkward infatuation with her can be called love. Tammy and I sat in her kitchen for the better part of an hour, drinking coffee, talking about our lives, Kristi, cancer, how much things had changed, and how much they had stayed the same. Despite the nervousness that had initially swept over me about seeing her, I was tremendously happy I had stopped in to catch up, to reconnect as only childhood friends can. Sometimes the best friends are the ones you haven't seen in the longest time, because their smiles bring back the kind of memories that last a lifetime.

With a sense of satisfaction and sadness at saying goodbye, I gave her a hug, and headed East towards Halifax, Nova Scotia. It was raining again, the wind was blowing, and it wasn't a great day for driving, but the highway was clear of traffic and the 4-hour drive would be over in no time. I was on my way to see one of my oldest friends, Bill, his wife, Eva, and their three kids, Emi, Ken, and Willa.

This family holds an incredibly special place in my heart, as it did Kristi's, because I've known Bill and Eva since the late 80's and because we were also the godparents to their children. Kristi and their daughter Emi were best friends from the moment they met, and whenever they would visit, Kristi would plan special events and outings just for her and Emi. Whether it was shopping, crafts, drawing, or simply cuddling on the sofa, she always seemed to light up whatever Emi was around.

Emi was the daughter Kristi never had, and she loved Emi as if she were her own. Fortunately, Emi was able to come and see Kristi just a few short weeks before she passed away, and she was also able to attend Kristi's Celebration of Life with her father Bill. I'm sure this had to be a tremendously sad and confusing time for a twelve-year-old. First, watching the woman she idolized become sick, going through her battle with cancer, then hearing of her situation, seeing her just weeks before her passing, and finally coming to grips with the fact that she was gone. I tried my best to give Emi a little piece of Kristi by building her a special shadow box filled with some of Kristi's favorite jewelry, as well as one of 15 pendants that contained Kristi's ashes, which she can wear around her neck or simply hold onto when she feels the need to be close to her memory. To know the love of a child that isn't your own is an unbelievably special thing, and Kristi and Emi shared a bond that is forever unbreakable.

I felt a tangible relief when I arrived in Halifax, and after two days decompressing with Bill and his family, it was time to spread Kristi's 8th bottle of ashes. On a cool, September Sunday morning, Eva and Emi accompanied Jake and I to the lighthouse at Peggy's Cove, Nova Scotia, a landmark that everyone should at some point in their lives visit and spend a few moments amongst the rocks and waves. This is the place we had chosen to spread Kristi's ashes, and the morning was beautiful. As the fog burned off, the morning sun shone brightly. There were very few people at the lighthouse that morning, so we practically had the entire area to ourselves. We found a wonderful spot to take some photos, and then I held out my palm to let the wind carry her ashes to settle among the rocks, and eventually, into the sea. It dawned on me at that moment that Kristi was a part of the Pacific Ocean, the Gulf of Mexico, and the Atlantic Ocean. Small fragments of her energy and her essence will float forever around the world, just as they will inside of me, and in everyone else she touched. I could tell that Kristi's energy was with me and always will be. There truly can be sunshine in mourning.

I stayed at Bill and Eva's house for a few more days, spending time with the kids, catching up, and getting ready to start heading Northwest towards my childhood home. I knew that going home wasn't going to be the same as it was so many times before, but I needed to feel that sense of connection that you can only get when you're back in the place where you're from. I did not have to drive the entire distance at once and had built an extra stop in the first leg of the trip to visit my Aunt and Uncle, then planned to travel North to see my father, and after a few days, West to see my mom and some friends in and around Toronto, Ontario. I was expecting to be back in Illinois the first Sunday in October. I think if I could, I would have extended the trip forever; but practicality, and a desire to sleep in my own bed, prevented that.

The next morning, I traveled over to the South-central part of New Brunswick, Canada, to visit my Uncle Evan and Aunt Gloria. I hadn't seen them in over twenty-five years, and yet, thankfully, it was like we had seen each other just yesterday. It was so good to reconnect with family. Even though the reconnecting was due to an unfortunate loss, it was still a relief to sit and share Kristi's story, our story, with them.

Where the waves crash ashore. Peggy's Cove, NS Canada.

Mourning is not easy to go through, but avoiding the pain of mourning means trapping yourself in a fantasy that can never become reality.   -Jonathan Grayson

While the visit wasn't long, it was enough to give me a sense that I need to hold on to things tighter than I have in the past. I had drifted away from my home over the years, and even at those times when I came back to visit New Brunswick, I rarely ventured out, and spent most of my time at my father's. I had become the person that I'd always scoffed at, the person who leaves home only to return for a quick vacation or when life has made a turn for the worse, forgetting that others might need you and what you represent to them.

I was returning home because I needed them, rather than because they needed me. I was returning home because, deep in my soul, I was aching for someone to tell me it was going to be okay, and that I wasn't crazy for missing my wife so much. That it was normal for there to be moments when I simply wanted to stop breathing. I yearned to reconnect with old friends and family, who I hadn't talked to in over thirty years, simply for the sake of shaking their hands, hugging them, and feeling the kind of warmth that you can only get from people who've known you since you were a child. My grief was so deep I was reaching out beyond the length of my arms in hope that I could gather from them some strength to get back home and figure out my life.

Pit Stop: House and Home

The decision to sell the house has been one of the most critical choices I've made in my life. While packing up the house at times seems cathartic, I fear that in the end I will regret making this decision so quickly. There are so many reminders of her. Little items of decoration, notes found tucked inside of boxes, things hidden in her office. There is a general sense that I am packing up our entire life. Not packing it up to be set aside for eternity but packing it up because I need to move it to some place that is safe for me to remember it. My house is not a safe place for me right now. It does not provide me comfort and warmth. It is a reminder of a time I can never recover, a time I can only visit in memory, and in time, I know, even that will fade. There is a weight in the pit of my stomach, and I hope, as I pack, as I feel it with every breath, with every little trinket I tuck away, that it will lessen in time.

Soon I will be taking photos of the house to get it ready for sale. This is another milestone that I never thought I would have to face alone. I don't want to sell this house, but I can't stay. There are too many memories, too much tied into it, so that even during the day when I have things to distract me, I'm uncomfortable being here alone.

I pretend that I like going out, but it's really that I dislike being home alone more. I've never felt this uncomfortable in a place, and it's unnerving for that place to be one where I used to derive such comfort. Maybe if we hadn't made this house into such a home, I wouldn't have as much of an issue staying in at night, but every inch of this house reminds me of a life I can't have back.

I know the pictures are going to go well. The place is going to look beautiful online, and I have no real worry that it will sell quickly. But I'm really scared about moving. It's not that I don't want to start fresh, and create a new life, it's just that there's a part of me that doesn't know how. If Kristi was here she could tell me, comfort me; that's just who she was. But now it's just me, and I don't feel like I'm making any ground. I feel as though everything is a challenge, a problem that needs to be solved now and I simply don't have the answers.

But despite that fear, despite the panic that paralyzes me, weighing me down with worry, I realize that I'm the only one that can make me better. So, I'm going to finish writing. I'm going to tidy up the rest of the house. I'm going to meet Michelle for photos, and take Jake for a run, and then maybe I'll convince myself that throughout this entire ordeal I'm going to be alright.

I look at houses online, but none of them appeal to me. In fact, I think there's a part of me that's terrified of actually buying something new by myself, because I know then it will be mine alone, and I won't have that shared memory. Even filled with my things, a new house will feel empty without her presence to fill it. This is so hard, and I'm trying to pretend that I'm okay, and I'm just not. I miss my wife so much that it aches. I would give anything to not have to think about other people, to not have to worry about dating, to not have to worry about whether I am impressing others. I just want her back. I want to hear her voice calling me from another room. I want to hear her footsteps coming down the hallway. I want to feel her kiss me on top of my head. I want to hear her tell me she loves me as my eyes fall heavy with sleep. Mostly, I just want to sit beside her, and be.

I can't feel her anymore, and it terrifies me.

I'm really grasping right now, stretching my arms out for anyone to hold on to, finding only dust. I don't think there's a single person out there that really understands just what I'm going through, and I don't know how to explain it to people anymore. I'm tired of trying.

I look at life as a novel, one that is never truly finished until we exhale for the last time. For as long as we live, chapters will continue to be written. It is never stationary, although at times it may move so slow it seems that way. We must resist the temptation to act, when we should be sitting quietly and listening. Moving requires a commitment to the destination. It eludes me still, like a salmon who refuses to approach a fly on a hot summer day. I cannot coax myself to sink the hook into my cheek, to take the pain and swim until the line goes taught. Am I ready to recreate myself yet again? Am I more afraid of what's behind me than what's ahead? If so, how do I turn that fear into action? As I explore the limited opportunities this once-familiar place still offers, as I examine what life would be like living once more along the banks of the Restigouche, I sit by myself with nothing but the wind and my thoughts and I feel nomadic, unsettled, afraid. Afraid of wanting something so badly it becomes a tortured reality.

Be careful what you wish for.

Maybe my life from this point forward is meant to be lived in multiple places? Is it possible that "home" for me is not as much about where I live, as where I am? I truly don't know, but as the wind whispers in the trees, and I stare out at a river that has always captured my fascination, I wonder if it's possible to be someone who's never, yet always, at home.

Kristi...I don't know what the future holds for me, but I do know this: I will stop crying. I will gain a sense of self love and appreciation. I will find joy and happiness, and I will be loved. I won't try to schedule or plan for all of these things, but I know they will happen. I know that some morning I'm going to stare out the window and realize that, while writing to you, the tears once familiar on my cheeks will not be streaming down my face in sadness, but in joy. I will be able to shout at the top of my lungs that I am okay, and mean it. I will be able to smile and embrace the world as it smiles back at me. I will be able to say, "I love you," to someone else, and, even more telling, I will long to hear it back in their voice, rather than in yours.

So today I'll continue to get this house ready to sell. I'll pack the pod so that everything is in perfect order, and I'll do the things I need to do to get through the day. I'll take what little packets of happiness I can and store them for when I need them, because that's what days are like right now. Each day will get better in some small way. I may not notice it, or even accept it, but healing is inevitable. There will be dates and anniversaries when the reminders are unbelievably strong and painful, and I will use those small packets I've collected to get me through them. And, in time, I will use the comfort of someone new as these days approach. One day, rather than fear those moments, I will greet them with a smile and the fondest of memories. I will let them wash over me like ocean waves as I bask in their sunlight

It's hard to describe a feeling you've never had before. I imagine it's like trying to describe what it's like to hear to someone who was born deaf. Right now, as I sit at the counter and write using dictation, the echoes of my own voice come bouncing back at me, the whispered ghosts of memory. The house is sold, and as of tomorrow, it will no longer be H&K House. The family room is empty, without a single hint that I was ever here except the hollow ring of my voice. Many of the rooms in the house are like this now; empty, dormant, waiting to come alive for a new family. I am not sure if what I feel is sadness or simply melancholy, but it is different, and the simple fact is this: despite all this house has meant to me, it is no longer mine.

If these walls could speak above my mumbled echoes they would tell tantalizing tales of a couple in love. Two young boys growing up. A mother whose love was boundless. Long summer nights in the backyard. Mouthwatering dinners, terrifying moments, tear-stained cheeks, and an endless bounty of courage and joy. They would share the hundreds of things we did to make it our home. The iron rocking bench on the front porch, the two red Adirondack chairs on the back step where we would sip coffee or wine, a home office meticulously decorated to provide not only functionality, but encouragement and motivation to a woman battling for her life. The dozens of mismatched knickknacks handpicked by the two of us, their significance an enigma to all but us alone.

So many people have enjoyed themselves within these walls. Friends and family, young and old, held us in this space, filling our lives and creating memories. Now it is someone else's chance to take this beautiful home and make it theirs. It's time for a new couple to sit out by the fireplace, for new friends to gather on the back patio, for new family to bond in the basement while playing pool and listening to music. It's time again for teenagers to laugh in the game room, to enjoy sleepovers and horror movies, and shovel the agonizingly long driveway as the snow drifts faster than you can clean it off.

As I say goodbye to these walls, my mind searches for the closure I've been seeking. Is the sale the end of the chapter? The entire story? What comes next? I have decided not to stay in Illinois, but to completely reset my life and move someplace else. I plan to take the next few months to decide exactly where I'm going, and then I will start over. I'm going to miss this house and all the memories we share, but it truly is time to take a leap of faith like I did 16 years ago. I am restless and need a change, a new opportunity, and now that all the boxes are moved, and the furniture is gone, I need to build up the courage to remove the last piece of clothing hanging in the closet: a simple white dress. Like me, for the moment, it no longer has a home.

I love you, Kristi. I miss everything we had together, and I'm trying to find a way that I can both miss it and cherish it. To hold it in my arms and know that the pain, while always present, is not a burden, but an indication of just how much you will always mean to me.

It's also hard to be at ease with yourself and the decisions you're making when you're unsure where you're going. As I sit at my father's house, my childhood home, I struggle to feel at ease with the changes that are coming my way. As much as I might want to, I know I don't just get to go "home" and restart life after being gone for 33 years. Things change, as do people, and places. The home I knew all those years ago is not the same. It hasn't necessarily changed for the worse or the better, it's just different. And while I find myself intoxicated at the idea of reacquainting myself with old friends and family, I need something more than the parade of hugs that I know will eventually end.

There is a gravity to the idea of going home in a situation like mine, but the act is not as simple as the idea. As the wind whispers amongst the trees along the banks of the Restigouche, I find myself asking, "Am I ready to bring myself back home? Am I ready to turn my back on what now seems like an entire lifetime? My friends, my career? Can I walk away from life as

I've known it and go back to a place which may eventually feel just as discomforting as the one I was leaving?" I just don't know. The lure of conversations with my father, fly fishing for Atlantic Salmon, winters filled with activity, and the all too familiar French-hinted accent of Northern New Brunswick are beguiling to say the least, but, life is not a Monet painting. There is more to it than the beauty we see on the surface.

I didn't realize I had truly lost my sense of "home" until it was gone. In retrospect, I guess at some point along the grieving pathway everyone starts to ask themselves the question, "is this still home for me now?" What I didn't realize was how important it is to know, deep down inside, where that special place you call "home" actually is. Maybe it's the sense of being a part of a place that's comforting, or the feeling you get inside when you're there, but the concept of being home is something I've lost, and I dearly want it back.

Home isn't just a geographic location or a building to live in, it's the special feeling a place gives you. And, even though there are times when I feel like I know where home should be, the act of finding my true home is a terrifyingly large task. Part of me believes I should take more time to figure out who I am, and why I'm here, before I figure out where home truly is; the other part says, "if you just choose somewhere, anywhere, things will all fall into place." Or will they? I know myself. Falling in place and falling apart have run parallel paths in my life. At any moment they can collide with catastrophic effects. Is going back to where I grew up running away? Is wanting the comfort of family and old friends an act of courage, or cowardice? What if they are both? What if what I truly need is more time under the stars in the RV with Jake, my thoughts, and a good bottle of red wine?

The Journey: Stage Four

I arrived at my father's in the middle of the day, and was saddened to see that his wife Patty, who had been undergoing treatment for stage four colon cancer, was not looking well. She was thin, pale, almost gray, and looked nothing like the strong woman I had grown to know over the years. Her cancer had recently spread to her lungs, and she was putting on a brave face, but I could tell that her time was running short, and that my father would soon be facing the same loss I had.

It's hard to say what I felt at that moment. Anger, fear, sympathy...these, and more, all fought within me, to the point where it was difficult to distinguish between them. Unsure, I said little, gave her a hug and spoke some words of encouragement knowing they would not help and focused on getting myself situated down by the water in the RV. I spoke to my father and asked what he needed me to do while I was there. I found myself immediately switching from wanting to be there for his support, to being there to support him. It was a role I was glad to take on, one that, in a strange way, provided a welcome distraction from my own pain.

The following morning, my father and I went out to pick up some firewood from a friend of his, in preparation for the cold winter months that Northeastern Canada is known for. When we returned, Patty's nurse told my father that an ambulance was on the way to take her to the hospital. She was concerned about some pain Patty was having in her abdomen, and felt it needed to be looked at immediately by a doctor. The ambulance took Patty to the local hospital, my father close behind, while I continued to work on stacking the wood. My father returned later that afternoon with dreadful news. Patty's treatment had come to an end; she had only days to live.

I did not feel grief, or sadness, or anger; not for myself. I just felt sad for my father. The woman he loved, with whom he had spent the last 30+

years, the woman who had become an irreplaceable extension of his life, just as Kristi had been for me, was going to die in the exact same way Kristi had. There were no more treatments, no magic cures. Just the slow march to death that cancers of the abdomen cause. I was not surprised, but as I silently cursed under my breath, I was comfortably thankful I did not have to reconcile my emotions with the idea that this was God's plan.

I did my best to console him, to let him know that I was there to support him. But deep down inside, I was aching so badly I don't believe I even said the right words. Again, I was confronted with the fact that I wasn't built to be a nurturer. I'm a doer, I'm a fixer, and I often find it difficult to be the person giving or being given a hug. I feel lost when my drive to solve a problem runs up against the immovable force that is fate, and now, I was helpless but for the words of advice I wasn't even sure were going to be helpful.

Over the next few days I did everything I could to guide my father. I tried to let him know what was coming at him, gently, but without withholding the truth. The terrifying approach of his wife's death was something I needed him to understand. Perhaps, in a way, I wanted to prepare him in a way that I was not prepared when Kristi's life ended. While nothing I could say would change the inevitable outcome, maybe in some way I could ease that transition for him.

I'm not sure he fully grasped what I was trying to do. I explained to him all of the things that were going to happen, the administrative tasks that needed to be taken care of: banking issues, notifications, property deeds, changing of names on accounts. And, on a personal level, how the loss was going to hit him at any time, on any day, at any hour, sudden and unpredictable. I tried to explain that there would be times when he would feel normal, and that life was going on; but that moments later, he would be wracked with grief and pain so deep he'd want to die to escape it.

I was also worried that he would drink. My father, like me, has a history with alcohol and has on more than one occasion been the victim of his own mistakes. Over the years he has developed a condition with his pancreas that forbids him from drinking alcohol in large quantities as it causes severe abdominal issues. But in times of grief, drinking often feels like an easy fix, a way to dull the senses, ease yourself to sleep, or allow you to be in a room with people when you'd rather not be terrifyingly alone – I should know.

When the time came, I went to see Patty. I gave her a hug and a kiss, told her I would take care of my dad, and sat with her for a time. I don't think she knew I was there, and the scene was eerily familiar. She was drifting in and out of consciousness, just as Kristi had in her final days, and I knew that time was short. When I left the hospital that evening I knew I would never see her again. I went home and spent the evening down by the river, its steady rhythm both soothing, and a bitter reminder that life would go on even when our whole world seems to have ended. I sat there for a bit with my father. He knew what was coming, and was trying to be strong, but I knew deep down inside he was absolutely terrified at the prospect of losing his wife and being alone.

Early the next morning the hospital called and asked him to come visit because Patty's condition had changed, and it was likely she wasn't going to make it through the day. After he left, I spent the rest of that day piling wood and making sure everything was taken care of so that he didn't have to worry about heating the house all winter. I tidied up and waited for a phone call. Around 5 p.m. I went to dinner at a local restaurant about a mile from where my father lives. I sat on their screened in porch overlooking the river and eating my meal when I received the call from my father. He simply let me know that Patty had passed away, and that he would be home shortly.

I quickly finished my meal and headed home. He was already there when I arrived, and I held onto him as he began to cry. There's something unsettling, almost terrifying about watching your parents cry. We're not supposed to see them cry, not supposed to see them break, or have moments of weakness. Yet, in that moment, he wasn't my father. He was a man who had just lost everything.

As he began to calm, I let him rest, and went back down to the river; my sanctuary away from everything. I made a fire and waited for him to join me. After a few hours he came down in an obvious state of intoxication, and while I was angry at him for drinking, I understood. His entire life had changed in an instant, and he was grasping for the one thing he knew all the while trying to mute the sadness and fear that was welled up inside of him. I sent him to bed and told him I would see him in the morning. As I went to bed myself, I felt utterly alone.

The Restigouche River is as much a part of me as my combined memories of childhood. I grew up on its banks, played, swam, fished, and spent summers in and out of the river until I was eleven years old. My father's house sits just up the hill from the river, and he keeps his camper right near the water. This is where my RV was parked while I stayed at my dad's, and where I am drawn to every time I am home. There is something peaceful about sitting on the banks of a river, something that nature does to you, to your soul. It has such a calming effect. The water slowly running over the rocks, down towards the bay, moving without a care of time or what's in its path. Kristi loved the view from my father's, and every time we were visiting we would always spend time down at the river or on the river in one shape or another.

I had hoped to spread Kristi's ashes in the river at a special place where we had camped years before, but unfortunately the water level was so low this late in the summer that it wasn't possible to reach. So, my father, Uncle, Jake and I decided to go to a place called Camp Harmony instead.

Camp Harmony is a fishing lodge where people from all over the world come to fly fish for Atlantic salmon during the summer months. As it was September, the main lodge was closed, but we were able to get down to the camp near the water. It wasn't a perfect day by any means, slightly overcast with a bit of a chill in the air, but the scenery, as always, was fantastic, and it was indeed a perfect spot to bless with some of Kristi's spirit, her essence. We spent some time at the river, talking about Kristi as we looked out at the water. And then, after a little while, I took the cork out of the bottle and I shared her with the Restigouche.

After that we were quiet for a bit. We took some pictures while I gathered my thoughts and my senses, allowing myself to feel the finality of placing Kristi's essence in another part of the world. A part of the world that also owns a part of me. My Uncle had built me a special box to put her remaining ashes in, so we brought it back with us, and it will make the perfect resting place for her. The box itself looks very unassuming. It's made with old barn wood, with leather hinges and it looks like it could have been used to store things in a hundred years ago. Just like Kristi's soul, it's perfect.

The next few days we went about making arrangements and helping my father get things ready for his wife's Memorial. Like Kristi, Patty didn't want a funeral; she wanted a Celebration of Life near the river where they spent most of their time during the summer and fall. Of course, being from a small town, the number of people that stepped up to help was incredible. After a few days, I was confident he was in good hands, and I was finally able to pull myself away and continue my Journey.

Finding some peace along the Restigouche River, NB Canada.

The drive from my father's to Toronto was difficult. I was feeling sad, lonely, as angry as ever, and listening to talk radio all day long while political pundits on both sides of the aisle argued the patriotism of kneeling for the national anthem did nothing to soothe my mood. I drove the entire day because I didn't want to stop overnight anywhere. I couldn't handle another night on my own. So, after 14 long hours, I arrived at my Aunt and Uncle's in the northwest suburbs of Toronto, where I planned to stay for a couple of nights.

My Aunt Patsy and Uncle Don have always been there for every major event in my life. They were there the day I was born, the day I graduated high school, the day I graduated from Military College, and they attended my and Kristi's wedding on October 12th, 2002. Of course, they were also at her Celebration of Life. If I could have chosen only a limited number of people to participate in spreading Kristi's ashes with me, they would have been among the few I would have asked to be with me.

I asked my Aunt to help me think of a good place to spread Kristi's ashes north of Toronto, the city I was born in and had lived on and off for almost 10 years in the 80's and 90's. She suggested that we use the Credit River. The Credit flows from north of the city down through Caledon, into Mississauga, Oakville, and finally into Lake Ontario. Its northern banks are a great place to sit and relax and get away from the hectic pace of Toronto, a place we had often visited to see my mother, members of my family, and Bill, Eva, and the kids. So, the following evening as the sun was beginning to set, we took Kristi's ashes up to this wonderfully calming place, and after wading into its midst, I spread them in the river, knowing that this was the last jar of ashes on the trip.

I think I was expecting there to be some sense of finality to it all, some sense of closure, and I'm not sure if I achieved that or not. Life isn't a Hallmark card or Lifetime movie, and our feelings and reactions aren't scripted. But there was certainly a moment when I realized that, for all intents and purposes, the reason for the trip was over. For the moment I was free.

A beautifully quiet spot on The Credit River, Ontario Canada.

The following day I after a quick stop to see my mom and make plans for the next two days, I traveled North to Georgian Bay to see an older cousin of mine and her husband. It had been years since I've seen Doreen and Bill, and the moment I saw their faces I was filled with memories. These two people had played an integral part in my teenage years, when we first moved to Toronto after my parent's divorce and didn't have a place to live. They took my mother, brother, sister and I in and let use live in their basement until we were on our feet and able to support ourselves. Catching up with the two of them was so much fun it was almost magical. Sitting on their back patio, catching up on years gone by, talking about life with Kristi, drinking beer, and occasionally laughing while Doreen scurried around fretting about dinner...for just a little while, I felt at home again.

A few hours later my mother and her boyfriend Neil arrived, and we sat long into the evening eating, talking, laughing, crying and enjoying each other's company. Unfortunately, I had to call it a fairly early night, the exhaustion from the trip settling into my bones in a way that could not be ignored. But I was awake bright and early at seven, so Jake and I could enjoy a good run along the Georgian Bay coastline in the cool September air.

After breakfast and some more conversation I decided to take the long way back to Toronto through the town of Wasaga Beach. My mom and Neil followed behind the RV, and after finding a good spot to park, we watched Jake play in the wind-whipped surf; chasing balls, jumping over waves and running down the shoreline as his tongue dangled back and forth. There is nothing more enjoyable than watching this dog in the water. He is completely alive, completely free, and you can tell just by looking at him that he is the happiest animal on earth.

We spent a good hour in and out of the water. Finally seeing exhaustion in Jake's eyes, I could tell it was time to head back to the city. I said farewell to my mom and gave her the biggest hug possible as they headed to their car. As they waved their goodbyes I drove South back towards Toronto for one last night. I was anxious to see an old friend of mine, who had been helping me along the way with dozens of positive thoughts and messages during the trip. I made it to a campsite in the city close to her place, and she joined me for dinner later that evening in the RV.

Sunrise on Georgian Bay, Ontario Canada.

Roberta is a very special person and someone I have known for almost 25 years. We lost touch in the late 90's, but she reached out to me when she saw me on social media and stayed in touch, checking in from time to time along the thousands of miles of my journey. Over the years she has a gained a sense of serenity and wisdom and has an understanding of human energy that I found very comforting. It was nice to just sit and talk with her about life, love, and the loss I was dealing with that evening. We could have talked for hours, but unfortunately it was a weeknight and she had work the next day. For the two or three hours we did have, though, I found myself comforted by her knowledge, her insights, and more of the gentle reminder that I was going to be okay at the end of this.

As I sit here now, I'd like to believe that. I'd like to believe that I am going to be okay, but there are moments when I honestly feel I am not. There are moments when I feel that the loss of my wife is essentially the loss of my life, and that nothing is ever going to replace her. That I will wander around aimlessly, pretending to be OK, in search of something better, something that I can never attain. I am sure this feeling will go away or fade with time, but what if it doesn't? What if it sneaks up on me unsuspectingly, just when I feel I have made it out of the forest and drags me back in?

"They say time heals all wounds, but that presumes the source of the grief is finite." — Cassandra Clare, Clockwork Prince

---

The last stop on my trip was a visit with some of my oldest friends, Rob and his wife Tammy. Sadly, we share in the common bond of loss. Their son was killed in a tragic accident almost a year before Kristi passed away. Because we had been in and out of touch with each other for the past few years, I didn't even know that Cody had died, and only found out after Kristi had passed. I was heartbroken to find out that their son, who I had held in my arms as a baby during their wedding, was no longer with them, and I understood, at least to some extent, the pain that they were still feeling. So, stopping in London wasn't an option, it was a necessity. I needed to connect with people whose emotional attachment to the person they had lost was as fresh and real as my own, and that's what I got.

I spent an entire weekend with them and their other son, Kade, and even had the great fortune to have Rob's mother, Margaret, who was like a second mother to me in high school, show up the day before I left. Throughout the weekend we talked about grief, sadness, managing life when you lose someone, and even the idea of finding new love again. Tammy is a wonderfully candid person, and was able to bring out in me this idea that life is going to go on regardless of the pain, and that we need to learn to accept it. Despite losing their son, Rob and Tammy still get up every day and do the things that need doing. They have fallen and they get back up. They have cried rivers and still they are thankful for the life in front of them and the love they have for their living son, Kade. It was an inspiration for me then, and the memory keeps me going even today.

As wonderful and needed at the visit was, it was my last stop, and I was somewhat anxious to get home. Early on Sunday morning I made my way towards the highway, and after filling up with fuel, West toward Chicago. The 7-hour drive seemed to take forever. But as I passed each milestone of this familiar route, a trip I had made dozens of times when Kristi and I were dating, I knew I was getting closer. From crossing over the bridge between Sarnia, Ontario to Port Huron, Michigan, to the on ramp from I-69 to I-94, and the final stretch on Route 20 in Illinois, I was almost done, but I wasn't finished. I still had two jars of ashes with me; one for Hawaii, and one for Mexico, where a small part of both of us will always rest.

Sadly, as happy as I was for the journey to be coming to an end, I knew I was going home to a house that was no longer home for me. I remember rolling up the street, seeing the house, and feeling an emptiness. An emptiness that would never be filled, because I would never be able to look at this house the same way. At that moment, something in me must have realized that I needed to move on. I had just driven over 11,500 miles, spread 10 jars of ashes, visited countless people and places and as I finally pulled into the driveway, all I felt was a sense of finality and sadness, both of which I knew were as real as the day Kristi died. I could sense it. My journey wasn't over; it had just begun.

It's easy, after a loss, to confuse "moving on" with "pretending it never happened." Taking the time to sit with the memories is crucial to the grieving process. To experience the pain of the loss is the only way to find that you still have other feelings, too. And, maybe more importantly--to realize that that's okay.

Moving Forward

As I look back, it's astounding just how much I accomplished. I traveled thousands of miles, placing Kristi's ashes in ten incredible places across North America. I cried more tears than I can remember, and I asked myself "what's next" countless times. I managed to keep my head above water and breathe during what can only be described as the most amazing Celebration of Life I'm sure I will ever witness. I opened myself up to the idea that life has more to give. I smiled at memories, had silent conversations with her ghost, and tried to look forward to my future with cautious optimism and hope.

Unfortunately, the one thing I don't get a do-over on is life with Kristi, so I had to take advantage of these opportunities in order to feel whole again. This trip needed to be done right, and the entire thought process behind it was a combination of healing for me, sharing of her, and the hope that when I returned home I would be more whole than empty, that my glass would be half full instead of dry, that my heart would be able to move forward one day at a time without feeling like it was being broken every second of every day. This process isn't easy, and there are days when I feel like I am completely empty; but there are also days when normal is right there in front of me, and as I reach for it it's just out of my grasp. That was Charleston. While it was out of my grasp that day, I will go back with clear vision and a more thought-out plan to give Kristi back.

In the meantime, I contemplate the future. The heart is a much more complex organ then we let on. I know my wife wants nothing more than for me to be happy, to go on and find a new life, a new partner, someone to share life with and to be as happy as I was when I was with her. But it's extremely hard to convince my heart that's the case. So, I did my best to put myself in a state where I could move forward. None of this is easy, but I believe the key is in how you define "forward" for yourself. To have a clear picture in your mind of where you're headed, and what the destination looks like.

To me, moving forward is having a day where I'm comfortable inside of myself, knowing there's something missing. This isn't something that comes easy to me, or to anyone, I suspect, and it's something I struggle with on a daily basis. In some ways I have struggled with it all my life. This idea that I can be whole, and at the same time missing something, is strange. There's always going to be this chasm or void that Kristi filled, which is now empty again, and somehow, I need to be able to reconcile that void with a future in which I'm happy. I need to find a new normal.

Now of course, having a day that's normal and being happy are not the same thing, but to me they're close. A normal day is one where I wake up and I don't feel this ache inside of me. This ache that says you're alone, Kristi is gone, and you must find your own way in this big, overwhelming world that has forever changed. A normal day would be one that's clear, one where I wake up and have a series of activities planned, work to be accomplished, dinner plans, and the comfort of knowing that when I go to bed the darkness in the room envelops me like a blanket rather than engulfing me, suffocating me, like ocean waves in a hurricane.

Normal would be believing in the direction that I'm moving. Normal would be having my drive and passion for life back. Both of which seem to have slipped through my fingers like sand. Normal would be wearing more than the same five outfits I seem to have settled on in the last month. And normal would be looking forward to seeing someone special in the evening, and quite possibly the next morning.

I long for normal. I long to be my old self, though I know I've been irrevocably changed by her love and by her loss. I want to get back the fire that Kristi fell in love with, because I know it's inside of me. It's been tamped down to the point where I don't recognize it anymore, but it's there. Many people have told me that I need to be patient, that time heals all wounds, and many other anecdotal catch phrases which, while undoubtedly true for some, never seem to capture my experience or fill me with the comfort and confidence I crave. I believe one of the biggest healers of wounds associated with loss and grief are the things we the grieving say to ourselves. So, I tell myself that I deserve to be loved, I tell myself that I am a good person, and I tell myself that someday soon I will be happy. I know it won't happen all at once, but if I keep telling myself these things, I know I can convince myself they're true.

Another part of moving forward that eludes me is finding a new purpose. I would like to believe we all have a purpose, that we all have a reason for being at any given time in our life. This can be a series of small singular roles the universe has created for us, or a more all-encompassing purpose to define an entire lifetime. For some, their purpose might be to raise a family, care for the sick, teach children, or protect the innocent, while others may play small yet critically important roles in other peoples' lives. I know some who for me have been beacons, while others have been warnings - bright amber lights letting me know to stay away from them and everything they represent. In the end, big or small, positive or negative, I believe we all have a purpose, even if we don't know what it is.

For the past several years I believe my purpose was to make Kristi happy with the life she was forced to live after December 28, 2012. Despite the obstacles that life placed in our path, I was comfortable in the knowledge that I was doing what I needed to ensure her happiness. It didn't really matter what I did for work, what occupied my time as a hobby, or what the future held; it really only mattered that Kristi was happy. My purpose was to take care of my wife. To comfort her, provide her with love, encourage her to dream, push her to take risks, and provide the support she needed to battle cancer and live a fulfilling life, regardless of how much sand remained in her hourglass.

Now, as life continues without her, I struggle with the concept of my purpose. I am not the same person I was on May 25th, nor am I sure who I will become at the end of this journey. There have been dark moments where life had no meaning, moments of panic as I realized what being alone truly felt like, moments of fear while contemplating the unknown, and moments of sadness as I wrestled with the loss of such an amazing partner and my best friend. Kristi was quite possibly the only person who truly knew me, accepted all my broken pieces, and despite them, wrapped her arms around me on the coldest of nights and loved me with her entire heart. Moving forward isn't easy. It's necessary, but what if I have no purpose anymore? What if I am done? What purpose do I play moving forward?

In the end, I have to believe the universe is not finished with me, and that it has a plan. I may not have all the answers, or any for that matter, but I will figure it out eventually. I am conscious and self-aware enough to know my entire life has forever changed, and now that one purpose has ended, a new one will eventually emerge. I will find my purpose, and with it a happiness that goes beyond a forced smile as I climb out of bed and take on the day. I'm just hopeful I'll do so with some direction and an understanding of why I'm still here and she's not. There are days when I would gladly take her place.

Deciding to wake up, make your bed, and go about life, even when you have no idea what it's going to throw your way, isn't moving on; it's moving forward. I know I'm not doing it in a straight line, because half the time I don't have a clue what I'm doing. But I do know this: the path may zig zag, and I may stumble, and I may make choices that others don't agree with. But in the end, I will make my way forward. I believe most people do. The amount of time might be longer or shorter, the decisions different, the people who pop up or pop down my change, but in the end most people move forward. We take a chance and try on that 6th outfit just to see how it fits.

The simple fact is that I can question what the universe is going to place in my path next, or I can embrace what it brings my way with open arms. So, just as she would have wanted, I get up every morning, I make my bed, and I venture out into the day. A day that now has more sunshine than darkness, and a day that, while sometimes cold and short on daylight hours, is still a day I'm learning to love and appreciate. This is what time does; it allows us to move forward and gives us the belief that if we let enough of it pass, we, too, can be whole again.

When your spouse dies, your entire life is flipped upside down all at once and every single day from that moment forward is going to be nothing like you've planned. At first will come the shock of what's happened, then the taking care of things that are unavoidable and necessary like memorials, notices, phone calls and a million other items that require your attention.

After that, if you're me, you will look for some deeper meaning in life and all the things that have happened in an attempt to escape the fact that you're now alone...completely alone. You are alone when you wake up, alone when you go to sleep and alone in making all of the life decisions you once made with your wife. It is a feeling so dark and encompassing, it can engulf you in an instant while it simultaneously tries to drown you.

As if that wasn't enough, the loneliness will be compounded by downpours of fear, anger and uncertainty while you try to move forward with your life only to be punched in the face by songs, photos, memories and the knowledge that nothing is going to bring them back. There is also a good chance your spouse's family and friends will begin communicating with each other about you, but not to you. Some may even begin questioning your decisions, words and intentions in hushed tones over coffee or via messages with one another. They might demand you justify your actions as if they somehow have a say in how you live your life and sadly, as is often the case, attack you about finances, wills, trusts and inheritances. Few may even go so far as to try and poison people against you in order to make themselves feel better about walking away. Discovering this can be devastating to some, but upon reflection it truly should be seen as a blessing. True feelings have a way of coming out in the end and the sooner the Universe reveals who belongs in our lives and who doesn't, the better it is for everyone.

You see, "they" (parents, children, siblings, friends and relatives) don't have to deal with the loss the same way you do at all. They don't have to erase every plan the two of you made for the future while trying to live and figure out what to do next. They don't have to go through every item you own and decide whether to keep, sell or throw it away. They don't have to make major financial and life decisions because the one person you intended to spend yours with is gone forever. Certainly, they must grieve, but they get to go on with their own lives with one (albeit important) piece missing from it, while you try and redefine the entirety of yours sitting alone at the table, trying to maintain your sanity while a myriad of voices and emotions scream and compete for your attention.

You will discover who your "family" and "friends" truly are and this can be uncomfortable and unsettling. You may curse more often and openly than you ever imagined (something I am quite good at and find deeply enjoyable and calming)...at people you thought were your friends, people you cared about and people you have given everything to over the course of many, many years. You may, in fact, even curse yourself in moments of weakness and fatigue as you try and piece your life back together without screwing up so badly that other people get hurt in the process.

If you're like me, you might crave the start of your new life while waiting for the old one to finally come to a close. Your current work or career may become meaningless, you might throw around hundreds of ideas about what to do next all the while being trapped in a house, city, state, etc. you both love and completely and utterly despise at the same time. You may go about the "life" you're stuck in and dream of a fresh start and "living" someplace else, anywhere else; going to dinners, smiling, laughing and doing all the things people who haven't lost someone do, while secretly waiting for your epiphany. Waiting for that moment when you can quietly sit down at the end of the day and say, "I've made it, I'm through". Yes, the death of a spouse or partner is "different" and something I wish I knew nothing about, but now that I do, I hope those of you who read these words understand a little more clearly that you don't just lose a "spouse or partner", you lose your entire life when their last breath is drawn.

Nothing compares, nothing at all, but how we choose to go on afterward is a choice we make not seeking acceptance or sympathy, merely understanding.

It's December 30th today and I, like all of you, am in the middle of the holidays. I'd been told many times the holidays can be tremendously depressing for someone who's lost someone like I have, so I decided several months ago I was going to do something about it. Rather than sit at home staring at the walls and mourning the loss of Kristi by myself, I returned home to Eastern Canada for Christmas. From December 20th - 27th, I was surrounded by family, friends, snow and love, creating what I have called "perfect distractions" for myself and my father. Distractions that served their purpose in more ways than one because they helped me realize happiness isn't just the destination when you're grieving, it's also a choice. A choice I get to make every single day.

Sitting alone, painfully soaking in old memories, regretting words not said or actions not taken, don't serve a useful purpose (at least for me). Choosing positive distractions and choosing to be happy with those memories serve a purpose. The conscious ability to reflect on something you've lost while at the same time choosing to step forward into the light and be happy is, in my belief, a major part of grief. It's OK to be sad, it's OK to miss someone, it's OK to cry, too miss moments and long for old conversations, just like it's OK to smile, laugh, look forward to the future and make choices that affect you positively.

Everyone at some point in their lives is going to go through grief. I had no idea how I would react to Kristi's passing, but in retrospect I think my behavior and the actions I've taken have on one hand been predictable, while on the other a bit surprising - at least to me. You see, I've at times been challenged when it comes to my own happiness. I've always had this foreboding sense that at any moment I will be overcome with anger, resentment, unease and feelings of unhappiness. So... it's surprising to me that somewhere along the way I realized I get to choose whether I'm happy or not. I chose to be happy over the holidays. I chose to visit my father and family in Canada (something I hadn't done in 17 years) knowing subconsciously I was going to be so occupied and distracted, I wouldn't have the opportunity to fall into a pit of tear soaked, holiday grief and mourning.

Certainly there have been moments of sadness and times I've reflected on everything that has happened this year with tears in my eyes, but in making the decision to focus my energy on positive things and thoughts rather than negative ones, I have been able to avoid the all too common depression people in my situation often experience . I don't know if any of this is "right" or if by some strange turn of events I'm actually running away from grief only to be smashed in the face with it months down the road, but I think this might be an exercise worth trying to anyone who's even in a remotely similar situation. We can choose to be happy, we can choose how we react and we can choose how long we want to sit in our grief versus taking the positive from life, standing up and moving forward (not "on") into the future.

Late yesterday as I was preparing dinner, snow was falling and it was simply beautiful outside. I don't often take the time to notice the beauty in life, but when it was brought to my attention just how wonderful my backyard looked in the fading light of day while snow fell to the ground and covered the trees, it made me smile. I was happy the universe had decided now was the right time for me to see just how beautiful my patio is in winter time. I was happy Kristi and I worked so hard at creating this wonderful backyard. I was happy for all of the long-lost family and friends I'd reconnected with over the past 7 months. I was happy for having a best friend who was willing to give up Christmas with his family to help me get through mine. I was happy that even though I don't quite know what the future holds for me, I'm OK with uncertainty and I was happy that my relationship with Kristi was so amazing and life changing I'm able to smile both inside and out without her as I embrace what's next.

Tomorrow is New Year's Eve. For many it's a time of celebration as they look back on an amazing year, a series of accomplishments, new love found or any other number of wonderful things that may have happened over the past 12 months. For me it will be a time of reflection. I'll take the opportunity to look back at 2017 and do my best to take positive direction from all that has happened. I will choose to look at the glass as half-full and if I cannot see my glass is half-full I will change the size of my glass so that it is! I will gaze forward into the future searching for moments when the light is fading and the snow is gently falling in life and thank Kristi for 17 incredible years. I will bask in the memory of her heart stopping smile and know she's smiling back at me somewhere, somehow.

I will choose to be happy. I have no other choice....

What She Would Want

The first time I laid eyes on Kristi, I knew there was something special about her. We met at our corporate head office in June of 2000 as she stuck her head over her cubicle and scolded me for being a smoker. The scolding could not have been more than five seconds, but five seconds was all it took. I was lucky enough to see her again at a sales meeting two months later and, like a smitten puppy, I followed her around for three days. Never in my entire life had I been so consumed with another person. Twenty months of dating, living 500 miles and an international border apart; dozens of weekend drives from Toronto to Chicago; it was an adventure in persistence, and the most amazing time of my life. If I close my eyes, I can still remember the blue flower print dress and sandals she wore the night I fell in love with her. She had me from the start, and never once let me go.

And so, as I start this process of putting myself out there, with the hopes that I find that someone who makes me smile inside and out again, I wonder what would Kristi say? What would she do if she were in the same situation? I know she dated during her separation, but this is different. This isn't a divorce; this is me moving on with my life, without her. And, never having wanted to do that, part of me wonders if what I'm doing is okay. Am I going to be in conflict with myself if I have feelings for someone else? Am I going to wonder whether Kristi would have approved of her? Am I going to have guilt with regards to the boys?

I think the human need to be close to somebody, outweighs everything. And I know that's what Kristi would want. I remember a few short conversations we had before she passed away, and the thing that resonates most with me most was that she repeatedly said she wanted me to be happy. She knew me and she knew I wouldn't be happy unless I was with someone else. I'm not designed to be alone. While some are destined to live a life of complete happiness by themselves, and others continuously search for the next best thing, there are also people like me, who want or need to be part of a whole.

I didn't realize this until not long ago, as I looked back on my life as an adult, my behavior in my twenties, the hundreds of therapy sessions I've had, and my life with Kristi. I was never so happy than when I was with her. I was never so fulfilled in my life then the moments when I felt the two of us were at our closest, and I was never so content as when I was beside her. We were fiercely loyal to one another, and in that loyalty our relationship was unbreakable. She was my best friend, and she knew me like nobody else does. She knows I'm not happy right now, alone, and she knows what it will take to make me happy again. So, I know that as I step into the future, and I begin to see other people, I will do so with her blessing.

I don't want her soul to worry about me. I don't want her energy to be consumed with helping me find whatever it is that comes next. I want her energy to guide my search, and I want to believe the next person in my life will have her ultimate approval. I believe I know what Kristi wanted for me, and it was for me to wake up in the morning with a smile. It was to look forward to spending the day with someone special. It was for me to desire to reach out and hold someone's hand as we walk down the street, and it was for me to make love to somebody new, to *want* to do so, knowing that I'll never make love to her again.

The next person in my life will always be second, but at the time they will be first. They will enjoy a place in my heart that nobody else has, but with the understanding that a portion of my heart has already been given away and can never be gotten back. I believe there's this small piece of me that belongs to Kristi in a way that is indescribable. I fell in love with her almost the moment I met her. I remember how it felt talking on the phone all those years ago. Messaging each other, emailing, long conversations. Traveling to Chicago to see her. The anticipation of a visit, of a kiss, of our first time together, and I know she wants me to have that again. I loved my wife to the ends of the earth and I would have traveled to those ends for her. Now I know that she wants me to find that same passion with someone else. With someone who isn't her but has a little bit of her inside.

"You said move on, where do I go?"
— Katy Perry

If grief is a path, then love, acceptance and happiness are its final destination. I'm learning that I must be willing to grieve and mourn for someone I've loved dearly, while at the same time open to finding happiness. I'm also learning I must be willing to engage in life and possibly someone new, while at the same time grieving for my loss. None of this is easy, and it requires a significant amount of self-awareness and understanding, but it is possible provided you understand a few important things:

New emotions do not erase old emotions. Hearts are fragile, yet capable of being rebuilt. Wounds do not need to be totally healed to venture out and explore. There is no such thing as a happy <u>and</u> lonely person. And the only voice that matters in the end...is yours.

Do I always feel or understand the direction I'm being pushed in? No. But I believe the decisions I'm making are based on the idea that this is what Kristi would want for me. To manage my grief in a positive manner, to find and create a life that's fulfilling, to celebrate our love and share it with the world, and to be happy as I eventually learn to love myself, and love someone else as I loved her.

One thing I know for certain is that my life isn't over, and what I need to really get my arms around is the fact that I have a new life that has just begun. Oddly though, there's some shame in moving on, and I need to address it so that I don't overlook the fact that it's there. There's a part of me that feels guilty for feeling good, and I'm sure I'm not alone in this. In fact, I'm sure millions of others have gone through the exact same thing, but you don't read books on grieving until your immersed in it, so no one ever told me this would happen. No one ever told me that happiness after loss comes with a price tag. It can make you feel dirty, ashamed and confused as you deal with the toll these conflicting emotions create.

I'm the kind of person who figures things out on their own, for good or for bad, and lives with the consequences of my actions. I can't say for certain I have any idea of whether I've done anything right in the last six months, but what I can say is that for the most part I feel like I've done what I've felt was right at the time. That being said, as I now look forward to a more positive future I feel horrible that that future doesn't include Kristi. I'm having difficulty looking at her picture on my wall because there's a part of me that feels like I failed her for not being consumed by my mourning longer.

I don't know if this is a normal response to grief, or one that's just me, but as I begin to feel better there's a part of me that feels worse, because I feel better, even okay, without her. It's hard to come to grips with the fact that I can be happy again without her, when just a short time ago she was everything to me. How do I reconcile the contradictory thoughts and emotions in my mind? How can I be happy and sad about the same thing at once? How is it possible that I can be positive about tomorrow and sad about yesterday at the same time?

Now I am torn at the idea of someone else staring me straight in the face, asking me to take her hand and move forward, while the other part of me is reaching back to cling to Kristi. To my memories, to 17 years of love. I'm afraid to let go of either. I'm staring at two worlds: one that could potentially be the future, and one that defined everything I am today. How do you let go without physically letting go? How do you pay tribute to something when you can't have a conversation with it? How do you look at old pictures and dive deep into the memories they evoke, while at the same time wanting to capture new pictures of today? How do you tell someone who isn't here that you miss them even though you're with someone else? How do you explain that you never ever want to replace the person that's gone, but you desperately want someone new beside you?

I can't run to a ghost, but I won't run from one either. No one said this would be easy, but no one ever told me how complex the interplay of emotions would be.

Many people in our world mistakenly call this guilt. Wishing that things could somehow have been different, better, or more is not the same as feeling guilty. If we do not identify different, better, or more, we begin to make the death or other loss responsible for how bad we feel. As long as we believe that someone or something else is responsible, we're unable to recover.

-John W. James & Russell Friedman, The Grief Recovery Handbook

---

How do we find someone new while at the same time honor and cherish what we had for so many years? I believe this delicate balance can only be accomplished through honesty, open communication, and understanding. In order for that to happen, your next "someone" needs to be aware of your grief. So, to the woman who becomes my next someone, here are a few things you should probably know:

You can never replace Kristi. I will never ask you to try.

Eventually, you will meet some of her friends and family. Don't worry—they will treat you with the same kindness and respect she would have.

There will always be pictures of her and our life together in the house to remind me of everything we shared. Pictures of you and I will be added as we write our own story.

There are things Kristi and I did and experienced together as a couple that I will want to share with you. Please understand they in no way diminish the things we will do and experience together. They complement them.

The love I will have for you is different than the love I had for her. It is not greater or less; it is simply different. Every couple loves in their own way.

Please don't try and compare yourself to her. You will be loved for who you are, not judged for who you aren't.

At some point I am accidentally going to call you by her name. Please take it as a compliment.

A small part of me will always be in mourning, but I know I can love someone completely while a part of me misses her.

I wouldn't be with you if I didn't think she wanted us to be together.

Love,

H

There's a hidden magic about the way you feel when you're in a place with someone you care about. Kristi and I could be anywhere, and I would always be comfortable by her side or across the table from her. I want that feeling again someday. I want those moments where you reach across a table while having dinner and gently touch each other's hands, those moments when you're in a booth sitting closely together talking about the things you need to do tomorrow, those times on a lazy Sunday morning when you're in bed together, listening to each other breathing under a pile of warm blankets. These are the moments that define relationships; these simple intimacies.

Intimacy, to me, is essential; it's a way for two people to connect through their bodies, through gestures, that goes well beyond the spoken word. Intimacy can be something as simple as feeling a set of fingers behind your ear as you drive down a country road, as gentle as a light touch on your shoulder while sitting at the kitchen counter, or that playful out-of-nowhere hug from behind when you're standing in a room. Intimacy is vitally important in a relationship, and when you've lived with it for 15 years, the craving to have it again is immense. It isn't about sex or passion; it's about human nature, and the longing and desire to feel connected to another person.

I am sure people who are grieving struggle with separating intimacy and sexuality—I know I have. But a healthy desire for intimacy is not something anyone should be ashamed of, and in fact, I believe it's something that simply proves you're human.

Defining intimacy is important, and for each person that definition will look slightly different. For example, to me, a crucial part of intimacy is conversation. It's one thing to talk to yourself about life, love, the future, and happiness, but it's another to talk to somebody else about all those things; someone who shares those goals, those fears and worries. Or, at the very least, someone who will hold your hand as you explore them.

I loved my wife more than anyone in the world and miss her terribly. I do not approach moving forward lightly, or with any sense of malice towards anyone else in her life. I believe I have the right to feel whatever I feel in the wake of my wife's death. And that includes an incredible sense of loneliness. It includes the ache to be held again, to be touched again, to experience the kind of love we shared - again.

Kristi and I shared a wonderful closeness and intimacy throughout the entirety of our marriage, but after her preventative hysterectomy in late 2011, and the completion of her debulking surgery in January of 2013, there was a dramatic change not only in Kristi's desire for intimacy, but in her ability to be physically intimate. And while I sit here with tears in my eyes describing this, I can only imagine the conflict that must have been going on inside of her. In fact, I recall the last time we truly made love. It was two days before her surgery in January of 2013. She was so scared of the idea that we might never make love again, that she summoned up every ounce of desire and for a brief moment, it felt like it was our first time. We were lying beside one another tears in our eyes, crying, terrified of what was next, but holding on to one another in a way that can only be defined by two people truly in love.

After the hysterectomy, multiple surgeries, chemotherapy, and the emotional strain and stress placed on my wife just to survive, not only was her drive diminished, but sex itself became painful and emotionally exhausting. Despite numerous attempts to combat some of the symptoms, we never truly regained our ability to be together like we did in the past. We were battling a mental war, a physical war, and at some point, whether conscious or unconscious, we were forced to adapt. I know how desperately my wife wanted to please me, but she simply wasn't capable, and I am sure this must have been devastating for her.

I desperately missed the kind of intimate relationship I had with my wife before cancer, but we accepted reality and embraced each other on another level. We replaced one type of intimacy with another, an increased level of caring, support, and kindness of one another. Our love never stopped growing during these years, and while we may not have enjoyed the kind and frequency of lovemaking we had in the past, we made love with our eyes, our voices, and the kind of intimate touches and embraces that go well beyond simple sexual desire.

You see, cancer didn't take anything away; it showed us what we had. And despite the toll it took on Kristi's body and mind, she never gave up, and she never stopped wanting to be with me. I can never thank her for that, but I only hope that her essence understands how much I miss her playfulness, and the look in her eyes when we were together. I grieve for the loss of intimacy between us, and I grieve for the fact that I will never make love to her again. So instead, I'll cherish all the moments I can possibly remember, every detail, the love she poured into our relationship, and I hope someday I feel the kind of connection we had again.

I hear a lot of people say, "don't make any major decisions in the first year," or, "you need to heal before you find new love," or, that "good things come to those that wait." But I don't want to wait. I'm alone while most of them are not. I want someone to hold my hand. I want someone to smile as I place a hand on their shoulder. I want someone to tell me that they're going to be with me through the good times and the bad. My love for my wife was deep, but I have so much more to give, and I desperately want to share it. Yes, I need to heal, and it's true that I need to grieve for the loss of my wife; but I won't let grieving stop me from finding my way forward.

I've often likened myself to a ship at sea without a rudder, but in truth it's much more complex than that. I'm not a ship at sea, I am a ship that's sinking because it doesn't have anything to buoy it up. My love for my wife and her love for me was the one consistent thing I could always count on over the last 17 years, and now that I don't have anyone to give that love to I'm desperately lonely; so much so that, like a person dying of thirst in the desert, I would drink the sand. I don't want a casual fling or something purely physical. What I want is someone who sees something in me just like Kristi did, someone who feels a connection with me that's so deep they can't understand it. I want someone who can count on me, and I can count on them. Someone who will touch my hand as they walk by or run their fingers through my hair while I'm sitting on the sofa. Someone who will whisper, "I love you," for nothing at all.

Friends and Family

I've had a bad habit over the years of walking away from people, places, and things and never turning around. I've moved several times in my life, and in almost every instance, I've just walked away and created a new life where I've ended up. My Aunt and Uncle reminded me, however, that family is forever, and while you may not see them every year, or talk to them every month, it's important to stay connected, because those connections are what make you who you are. They are the ones that own so many of the memories of you out there in the universe.

Whether they be forged by blood, or memories, or events that have shaped your life, connection is what binds you to others. I've had a long and complex history with my family, at times pushing them away, or simply letting them drift out of my life. Or, perhaps more accurately, I allowed myself to drift out of theirs, even doing a bit of paddling here and there to hurry the current along. I don't know if this is a common occurrence or not, but it's something I'm consciously aware of, and I'm thankful that in my time of grief they still wanted to hold me, to listen to and comfort me. Despite the distance, they wanted to be with me. And I found that despite the time, despite the past, I wanted to be with them too. That, to me, is family.

The first week after my return home wasn't exactly what I would call a disaster, but it was close. I was on edge, anxious, and confused—as was one of my stepsons, Andrew, who had chosen to live with me for a few months after his mother died and until he found a place of his own to purchase. While I am not sure, I think he felt I had selfishly abandoned him for the past two months to figure out my life, while he was left to mourn on his own. What he didn't know was that I wasn't taking care of my life, on this journey, as much as I was trying to do what I thought was best to honor Kristi and to find some healing of my own along the way so I could return and take care of my life. I was also escaping from reality for a while. I didn't have all the answers, nor did I have everything figured out. The true healing process, for me, was not in the journey; it had only barely begun, and even to this day is not complete.

Over the course of the first few weeks we had a number of discussions—a few of them heated—about life, grieving, his mother's wishes, and the situation we were now in. Our lives, while connected through Kristi and because we lived under the same roof, were separate; and I could feel us slowly growing apart with each passing week. But I simply didn't have the energy to try and pull us back together. I was barely holding onto myself and I believe a part of me felt that he simply didn't want to be in my life any longer.

Things seemed to settle down for a short while, but after finding a townhome and moving into a new place of his own—Kristi and I had agreed to use a portion of the life insurance as down payments for each of the boy's first homes—we communicated less and less frequently leading up to the holidays. I honestly didn't think much of it; we didn't communicate every day or even every week when he was in college and he had his father and twin brother and many close friends nearby.

Eventually, after the Christmas holidays passed, and I continued to move forward with life, the tone and content of his messages changed. He began to lash out, words and accusations were spoken that can never be taken back, and I decided to cut off all contact with him. At this point I believe nothing I can do or say is going to change how he feels, and sadly, I've reached the point where I simply don't care. I don't know if I will ever speak with him again, but I do hope he finds peace someday.

Everyone is different, and everyone handles the grieving process in their own way. For him, the loss of his mother at the age of 22 is not something he's ever going to get over. He is going to miss her at his wedding. He's going to miss her when his first child is born, and his second. At their graduation, and proms, and all those events children look to their parents for support and love. He is going to miss his mother's love for the rest of his life, something his father will never be able to make up for in all the support he can give. I hope he learns that she is all around him. That she is in the changing colors of the trees, that she is in the grass that grows every summer. She is in the love that he has for her, and the love that she had for him, and that she loved him more than any mother could ever love a son.

Kristi's boys were her life, and while I would like to believe I came first in her heart, it simply isn't the case. Her life revolved around her sons. Whether it was attending their sporting events, checking in on them to make sure they were doing okay at college, or simply being concerned about them for one reason or another, her thoughts always drifted back to her sons. It's hard to express just how much Kristi loved her sons, but I believe from the bottom of my heart she loved those two boys more than was humanly possible, and I say this without any anger or regret; I know that she loved them in a way that far eclipses the love she had for me. It was simply unmeasurable.

It's funny now, as I look back, because there were times when I was bothered by how much our lives revolved around the boys. Today, I would give those occasional feelings of jealousy back in an instant. I have drawn so much pleasure from the boys and the life that they have allowed me to live that I can only look up to the sky and thank this beautiful angel for what she gave me: an opportunity to be a husband, a step-father and her best friend. I will miss parenting with her, and I will miss discussing plans with her that revolve around the boys and their lives, but most of all I will miss watching her love her children, because nobody did it like she did.

"There are no stages of grief...Do not allow anyone to create any time frames or stages for you. There are no

absolutes in grief. There are no reactions so universal that all, or even most, people will experience them. There is only one unalterable truth: All relationships are unique." - John W. James, The Grief Recovery Handbook

---

Life changes after the dust settles. After the memorials are over life begins its daily drudge forward, whether you're ready for it or not. Of course, my situation was different, having taken two months to get affairs in order, and then another two months to simply travel with Kristi's ashes and share them with the world. But the end result is still the same. At some point you're going to wake up and life is going to be different.

One significant difference, for me, is my relationship with Kristi's friends and family. I no longer have any communication with my sister-in-law and her family. This was a very personal decision for me, and if the truth is told, it is one that came easily and one I am completely comfortable with. I was never truly close to her; our relationship was built out of necessity due to Kristi's illness and in her final days, caring for her as her health declined. After Kristi passed, I believe she mistakenly felt I needed her approval, that she had a right to judge my behavior, as if she was speaking for Kristi, when nothing could be farther from the truth. Some might say that it's sad, but in the end, this is what death does to people who are loosely tied together.

I still have a relationship with Kristi's other son, Bradley, and was happy to help him find and purchase his first home in March, just as his mother and I discussed before she passed away. I have done everything I can to ensure he has all he needs to remember his mother; every old photo, report card and scrap of paper from when he and his brother were young, her wedding an engagement rings so that he can one day share them with his future wife and I've let him know I am here if he needs me. Time will tell. As for others, I haven't talked with Kristi's parents much in the months since Christmas, because I do not want to become a wedge between them and the rest of their family. They all need each other more than I need them, and I am comfortable with the fact that I was Kristi's husband, and they were her family, not mine.

I have also come to grips with the fact that many of Kristi's friends, and people who knew her well, are not my friends. This does not mean in any way that they're bad people, or that I think poorly of them; they simply aren't or weren't truly my friends. They may be my acquaintances, or even former colleagues at work, but it's not safe to assume the relationship Kristi had with them is the same relationship I will have with them in the future. In fact, I have seen the majority of this entire group of people, with a few notable exceptions, quietly migrate away. I'm quite okay with this, because I'm not the kind of person who wants or needs a large group of people in their life and truth be told, all we have in common is the memory of my wife.

I am discovering that beyond grieving, there are other forces at play, some good, some bad and some that need to be acknowledged simply for their existence and ability to influence your life after loss. Some days you're going to wake up and everything will be just fine, while others will be different. You'll feel detached, alone, maybe even a little anxious...all of the things you thought you were putting behind you as you make your way forward. It's unsettling at first until you realize what's going on. You're in between the old and the new. The you who's life was "normal", predictable and balanced is gone and the you you're going to become has yet to be defined.

It's OK. Be uncomfortable. Sit still. Embrace the unknown and recognize that the future is ahead, not behind you and all days are not the same. You don't need to have it all figured out, but you do need to get out of bed and keep moving. Just because the skies are full of clouds does not mean the sun isn't shining!

I have also discovered that everyone who shared and loved your wife, husband, parent, etc...with you are going to react to your grief pathway in whatever way they feel is best for them (consciously or unconsciously). It is important to note that their grief isn't about you and your grief isn't about them. Everyone is different, has different relationships, different reactions to tragedy and there are a myriad of ways to grieve. It's a personal process, not a shared one and no one knows what goes on in your head, the thoughts you have in private or how hard you're trying to paint a picture of normalcy when life is anything but.

Some may not like you "moving on", they may not like you trying to be happy, they may not know what to say to you, they may want to dictate how you should behave and some may not want to be around you any longer for reasons of their own. On some occasions people may lash out at you over things that seem petty, selfish or even silly, but in the end it's important to remember they are grieving too. Your relationships with the people that were in your life are going to change, like it or not. There is no avoiding it, so watch closely who gravitates towards you, who begins to drift away and how you feel about each circumstance. In the end you will be just fine with the family and circle of friends you have left.

Where it gets more complex, though, is with those people who I believed I had a close relationship with, only to find that Kristi, like the woman of the same name in Kenny Chesney's song "Happy on the Hey Now," was the glue that held us together. There are several people I had always believed where my friends, too, even though Kristi had been the one that introduced us. Maybe this is naive, or maybe I'm reading too much into things, but I have come to realize, quite painfully at times, that there is no guarantee that anyone you were close to prior to losing someone will remain close to you afterwards. This is especially true with those people whose primary communication, history and contact was with Kristi.

Still, this is a realization I have come to accept. Am I disappointed with some people? Yes. Am I somewhat saddened that more people haven't reached out to me directly to ask me how I'm doing or to simply say hello? Of course. Am I sad enough that I will carry this forward? No. I've learned that the circle of friends and family that you hold dear to you are worth nurturing. You cannot rely on third-party relationships to help float you in times of despair. They aren't invested in you, they don't see a part of themselves in you, so your future and theirs are not intertwined because you do not have a shared history. More than anything, this experience highlights the need to cultivate relationships outside of a marriage or partnership.

I can count on one hand the number of people I would reach out to in a time of need. All of these are people with whom I have a strong long-term relationship with. Not a single one of them is someone I would classify as a "friend-by-proxy." In other words, a friend of mine because they were also friends with Kristi. My people are in places like Halifax, Nova Scotia; London, Ontario; Hampshire, Illinois; in Florida, and of course, home in the Northern reaches of Eastern Canada. These relationships have been forged in time, shared experiences, laughter, tears, and a bond that is unbreakable.

They are enough. And, for now, that is all I can ask for.

One Year Later

At 10:18 this morning it will be a year since we said our last goodbye. There was no note on the counter, no text message or the quiet hum of the garage door closing. Just silence. Yes...it's actually been a year since you drew your last breath, and since that time, this rock we all live on has traveled so far only to have gone nowhere. At moments, that's how I feel; that I've travelled so far and gotten nowhere at all. Just a year ago you were here in this place, quietly fighting to stay alive, and at times I feel I am doing the same.

The house, as you can imagine, is empty but for me and the dogs. The main floor is making its regular noises; the dishwasher is running, and of course there's a load of laundry in the washer. I have this thought that if I turn my head quickly, I might catch you standing at the foot of the stairs, looking back at me with your incredible smile and eyes that could see right into my soul. I miss that look, and all the ways your smile made me feel. Never once did I feel alone when I was with you.

It's been a year since I stood in a room full of what have now mostly become strangers, quietly waiting for you to take your last breath. Are you still here? Do you linger quietly, moving from room to room, watching me to make sure I don't give up? Do you keep your hand softly pressed against my back to ensure I keep going? I won't stop, I promise, but I will pause at times to see that I'm on the right path. There are times I wish we could go back in time with the knowledge I have now and do some things differently, but I'm not sure what that would be. In the end, nothing will have changed, and I will still be perched here writing to you a year later.

I'm desperate to start a new life, but a part of me is terrified. I know that as I start a new chapter, the one with you in it ends. I have memories and photos to hold onto, but a picture will never touch my hand, and I can't hear your voice in my memories. I've done my best to not let anger get the better of me, but there are moments when I just want to explode. People talk about grieving, sadness, and loss, while they hold onto memories and anniversaries, but they never mention the confusion, the anger, and the overwhelming sense of drowning when you realize there's so much to do in order to move forward.

I don't know what others who loved you have done these past twelve months, but as I sit here now by myself, I feel as though there is still a mountain of work in my path. At times my patience wears thin, but despite the frustration and the desire to be someplace else, somewhere I can call home, I sit and twitch while I wait for the universe to give me some direction.

This house, like my heart, is truly empty without you. But hopefully soon both will be filled with love and joy as they capture someone else's hearts and memories.

I miss you, Kristi. I love you.

Sunshine in Mourning

I lie awake in the darkness, staring at the walls
It's 3 AM and I'm restless, no I can't sleep at all
Memories about you, rush past me in a haze
I try to piece it all together, but it's been too many days
Are you happy with our new love, does Jesus treat you right?
Please send me a message, so I can sleep at night

Oh Kristi how are you? I haven't seen you for so long.
It's been 7 weeks now, and I'm trying to move on
But you, you're all around me, in everything I do
Even the air I breathe in, reminds me of you
Oh Kristi how are you? I haven't seen you for so long.
It's been 7 weeks now, and I'm not moving on

Somewhere in the distance, I hear the echo of a train
If only I could hop on, and ride away this pain
But your voice it haunts me, gently whispering in my ear
Taking me back to better times, to another year
And as a breeze slips through the window, I can feel it on my skin
Like the many times you kissed me, if only once again.

Oh Kristi how are you? I haven't seen you for so long.
It's been 7 weeks now, and I'm trying to move on
But you, you're all around me, in everything I do
Even the air I breathe in, reminds me of you
Oh Kristi how are you? I haven't seen you for so long.
It's been 7 weeks now, and I'm not moving on

My minds drifts back to places and times we shared before.
The love we had was so strong, it nearly knocks me to the floor
I catch my breath and senses, and wipe away the tears
And I remember how you loved me, all those amazing years
But nothing strips a man so quickly, so naked and so bare
As losing the one he loves, having to watching her disappear

Oh Kristi how are you? I haven't seen you for so long.

It's been 7 weeks now, and I'm trying to move on
But you, you're all around me, in everything I do
Even the air I breathe in, reminds me of you
Oh Kristi how are you? I haven't seen you for so long.
It's been 7 weeks now, and I'm not moving on

Now people always ask me, if I'll be alright
I just answer back politely, I'll make it through the night.
But as darkness approaches, and I lay me down to rest
I pray for you to haunt me, to feel your head upon my chest
I know the night will end soon, and I can hear the rain pouring
But, there's some comfort in the pain, some sunshine in the mourning.

Acknowledgements

To all of you who lifted me up when I was weak, who helped guide me when I was lost, and who let me be, when all I needed was the time to see things through. Thank you.

To Debbie, Robert, Melissa, Jim & Kathleen, John, Uta & Max, Erin & Ray, Gail & Steve, Nancy, Don & Carla, Tayler, Tim & Sara, Gene & Val, Jackie & Dave, Tom & Amy, Tammy, Lana, Bill & Eva, Jane, Joanne, Evan & Gloria, Dad, Sharon, Jill, Carol, Bonnie, Sandra, Charles & Tricia, Kevin & Patsy, Barb, Marjorie, Alsa, Angie, Butch & Kerwin, Natasha & Shane, Don & Patsy, Jody, Tara, Mom, Doreen & Bill, Roberta, Bobby & Tami, Amy & Ken, Jim & Kristi, Cindi, Connie, Beth, Kathy, John & Kristi, Jim & Janey, Mike & Theresa, Gerald & Sheri, Joelle, Dave & Stacey, Bud & Vicky and so many more who were there during the pit stops, the highs, the lows, and the tears as I waded through the memories of the last 17 years of my life one day at a time. While others were fading away, you were stepping forward.

To Julie & Steve – thank you does not describe how grateful I am for the two of you. The love you showered Kristi with in life and death was amazing. I do not have the words to say how thankful I am for everything you have done for her and for me. See you both in Florida soon.

To Jim and Linda – thank you for raising such an incredible daughter. You were truly blessed to have had a daughter like Kristi. I loved her with all my heart and would give anything to have her back if only for one more day.

Acknowledgements Cont'd.

To Brad and Andrew – your mother was a truly incredible person. She loved you without fear, cared for you with an amazing passion and wanted nothing but the best for you both. Whatever paths you take in life, she will always be there, watching, smiling and enveloping you in her love.

To Dr. Barbara Buttin – you are an inspiration. Thank you for giving her hope when she had none and the ability and desire to live in the face of fear. I will always be in your debt for all you did for my wife. She adored you!

To LivingWell Cancer Resource Center – thank you for all that you do for cancer survivors and their caregivers. You are what all cancer charities should look like.

Manufactured by Amazon.ca
Acheson, AB

11003431R00069